Cattle Cars to Heaven

by
Bernard Caron

Foreword by Kenneth Burg

Acknowledgments

A thankful appreciation is extended to our friend, Kenneth Burg, for offering his services in editing my original manuscript, as well as to my niece, daughter of my brother Jacques, Debbie Collins, for cleaning up any mess that Kenneth may have created.

Shalom to you and your families.

Dedication

To the memory of my parents, Maurice and Rachel, my brother David, my sister Sosia (Suzanne), and my sister Fernande; the world will never forget.

Table of Contents

Foreword

What good are the eyes in the light of disbelief? What good are the ears in irresolution? What good is communication if fact is rejected? General Dwight D. Eisenhower foresaw the potential of propagated ignorance as is true today. Despite the abundance of official documentation and firsthand testimony regarding the evils inflicted on humanity, sympathizers of a dictatorial regime continue to defend through denial the actions of Adolf Hitler, undermining the sufferings of the souls who perished at the hands of tyranny and insulting those survivors walking among us today. This gross disregard for life and insult of intellect must never be tolerated.

A war has been declared against the minds of each successive generation and truth itself.

Provocateurs and inciters of evil must be squelched by the active pursuit of knowledge and integrity to uphold what is right, all that is good and decent before man and Almighty God. Never before has the world foreknown tomorrow; history is written in the present as men decide what will be remembered. Let us never forget the atrocities inflicted upon mankind by tyrants, and let us never cower to their sycophants. Seek to know and do what is right by first hearing the testimonies of those who experienced what is now being pacified.

During the camp inspections with his top commanders, Eisenhower said that the atrocities were "beyond the American mind to comprehend."[1] He ordered that every citizen of the town of Gotha personally tour the camp, and after having done so, the mayor and his wife went home and hanged themselves. Later on, Ike wrote to Mamie, "I never dreamed that such cruelty, bestiality, and savagery could really exist in this world."[2] He cabled General Marshall to suggest that he come to Germany and see these camps for himself. He encouraged Marshall to bring Congressmen and journalists with him. It would be many months before the world would know the full scope of the Holocaust—many months before they knew that the Nazi murder apparatus that was being discovered at Buchenwald and dozens of other death camps had slaughtered millions of innocent people.

General Eisenhower understood that many people would be unable to comprehend the full scope of this horror. He also understood that any human deeds that were so utterly evil might eventually be challenged or even denied as being literally unbelievable. For these reasons he ordered that all the civilian news media and military combat camera units be required to visit the camps and record their observations in print, pictures, and film. As he explained to General Marshall, "I made the visit deliberately, in order to be in a position to give first-hand evidence of these things if ever, in the future, there develops a tendency to charge these allegations merely to 'propaganda.'"[3] Eisenhower's prediction proved correct. When some groups, even today, attempt to deny the Holocaust ever happened, they must confront the massive official record, including written evidence and thousands of pictures that Eisenhower ordered to be collected when he witnessed the aftermath of the Nazi's carnage.

Every soul is endowed by our Creator with identity and purpose. The significance of roles we undertake and niches we fill are intrinsically meaningful according the specific design. Man, however, sometimes deviates from an intended good, forging a path bent on destruction with intended or unintended consequences. The victims of such negligence happen to be situated with an opportunity to magnify the grandiosity of the God of Israel's strength as living monuments testifying of virtue.

Chapter 1

The Beginning

R ue de Dieu (God Street) was the name of the street in Paris, France where I was born. It didn't mean anything to me early in life, but eighty-four years later, I cannot deny the irony.

Adolf Hitler began to make waves felt all over Europe by 1933. He was ready for World War II while other countries were sleeping. In 1938, he demanded Austria, which he took over without resistance from other countries. He then demanded Czechoslovakia a few months later. I was not mature enough at eleven years old to understand what was happening when Hitler made up his mind to conquer the world. I stood on Rue de Flandre, watching Neville Chamberlin, prime minister of England, and Edward Daladier, prime minister of France, and other heads of state come together to hand over Czechoslovakia to Hitler on a silver platter. A few months later in 1939, Hitler demanded Poland, which I believe the allies, France, England, and other countries, were ready to concede. Poland, however, did not cooperate as easily. After months of negotiating, Hitler's army attacked Poland on September 1, 1939. The next day, England declared war on Germany, then a day later, France followed suit. I guess I was still too young to understand the potential impact these events would have on my family.

Poland's stand was short-lived prior to being completely overtaken by Hitler's army, which continued fighting smaller neighboring countries. In Paris, the general population was not concerned about Hitler. Everybody talked of the impenetrable Maginot Line. My father was not so optimistic. There was a lot of banter about Nazi conduct toward Jews in occupied countries, but these rumors were unconfirmed. Although based on the news we read in the papers and what we saw in the cinemas, Hitler's largest enemies were the Jews. His hatred for us was unbelievable. We were a parasite driving him insane. Still, radio and newspaper reports claimed that France and England were so strong that Germany would be defeated with nominal effort; hence, complacency lingered and life went on unwittingly, but I think the Jews were more concerned than others.

On Sunday mornings, my father would usually go to the Belleville Quarter where other business folk would meet on the boulevard to discuss their trades and the goings-on of the war. I loved going with him because after meeting with his friends, we usually ended up at the delicatessen. I would get the cheese-cake with the brown crust on top. I enjoyed the deli-catessen the most, but I learned much by listening to the conversations, benefiting me years later.

Everyone believing the war would end quickly was fooled. Hitler's army seized countries one after another with little opposition. None were ready for war except the Germans, who had begun to produce war materials as soon as Hitler came into power in 1933. This maniacal individual wanted to conquer the world. At the end of winter 1939 and in early spring 1940, German forces continued their expansion and began to hit their stride. Within one week's time Germany overtook the Netherlands. They arrested practically the entire Jewish population and nobody seemed to know of their whereabouts. Other non-Jews were forced to work in German factories.

Belgium was the next target and surrendered two weeks later. At that time, the fears and anxiety of the people in Paris escalated. Hitler could not be wished away and became a serious threat to France. A few days after the fall of Belgium, Germany attacked France. The Maginot Line did not hold as predicted, and the German Army was free to advance into Paris. For a while the Germans found some resistance from the French, but Germany launched a major offensive attack in early June.

I remember a few days before Paris fell, friends begged my father to take us and flee to England, and he actually decided to buy a small plane that would get us out of Paris. My mother was also expecting another child at this time. Yet, a couple of days went by, and my father changed his mind. He said, "I worked all my life for what I've got and nobody is going to take it away from me."

Bernard (Bernie) as an infant

Chapter 2

Home

Charles Lindberg flew across the Atlantic in 1927, creating worldwide pandemonium the year of my birth. I was the third of what would be thirteen births and ten living children.

Employment for Jews was not easily attained. My father (mon pere, as I called him), Maurice Choroszez, was a self-employed shoe cobbler in Paris. He rented a very small store between a tavern and a machine shop. The day I was born, February 15, a very large piece of equipment was delivered to the machine shop. The owner solicited my father's help, being without sufficient manpower to unload the heavy equipment. While unloading the truck, the equipment slipped and pinned Father's neck to the pavement. Bystanders rescued him from near death. He was badly bruised but recovered. I was fortunate not to be fatherless from the first day of life.

My parents were Orthodox Jews. I remember my father praying for an hour in private quarters every morning at six o'clock. He was ambitious and worked about twelve hours a day. He often said, "Every time we have a new child, I get richer."

My mother (ma mere), Rachel Choroszez, never worked outside of home; she always had her hands full taking care of us. She had a baby practically every eighteen to twenty-four months. I remember her as a devoted wife and mother. I have fond memories of my mother on Fridays going to the kosher market and buying food for Shabbat. She would pick out a live chicken, and the shochet (a ritual slaughterer) would slaughter it and pull the feathers off; my mother would finish cleaning it. She made her own gefilte fish (fish patty), chicken soup with noodles, and trimmings for the meal from scratch. While cooking, she cleaned the apartment, getting on her knees to scrub the floors—by herself! I don't know where the energy came from to do this alone. She would wash the walls and change the dishware, replacing them with kosher ones just for the eight days of Passover.

My father was the disciplinarian, with whom I was well acquainted. You could say I was a little leader with my friends; however, I had a hard time completing tasks that were required of me. Of course, I knew that I had it coming, as I was not always a well-behaved child. When I was six or seven years old, on my way home from school, a bunch of us kids began jumping up on the hood of a parked car. To this day I cannot recall whether I joined them, but the owner of the car approached my father and informed him of my behavior. I guess some of the other kids offered my name and address. Subsequently, the owner threatened my father with a civil suit and police involvement if he didn't pay for the damage. My father lectured me but without punishment because I was too young to understand the gravity of my actions.

I can recall another incident that occurred a couple years later. We had a lot of homework every day, and I studied by memorization. One day at school, I was called to the front of the class to recite what I had learned, but my mind went blank standing before the class. Not a word was uttered, so the teacher told me to return to my seat and gave me an "F." I insisted that I knew the subject and pleaded for another chance. He consented. But again, when I got to the front of the class, my mind went blank. Again he told me to return to my seat. I was so upset that I called him a filthy name. He heard what I said and challenged me to repeat myself, so I did. He handed me a sheet of paper, directed me to a seat in the last row of the class, and told me to write down the exact words that I said. I stubbornly decided not to. He said I could not participate in class until I wrote it down, but I resisted. My brother David was in the same class, and he begged me to write it; I still would not. After thirty days of stubborn resistance I finally gave in, so I wrote the words and handed the sheet to the teacher. He had a scrapbook started several years back and placed my paper within. I was then able to continue with the class.

After the war, I ran into him, and we became good friends. He even bought some shoes from me.

Ma mere, Rachel Choroszez,
and mon pere, Maurice Choroszez

We lived within the Nineteenth Arrondissement of northeast Paris in Belleville, a predominately Jewish quarter, in a building that was several hundred years old. We had an apartment on the third floor with four rooms. The bathroom was in the hallway one floor below us. My mother's cousin lived one floor above us, and he too was a shoe cobbler but without the opportunity of self-employed.

As our family grew, so did my father's business. It wasn't long until he opened his own retail shoe store in La Villette and hired a friend as a cobbler. When the family had grown to seven living children, we moved into a five-room apartment that became available above my father's store. The child born after me, Henry, had died of pneumonia, and my mother lost two other children shortly after delivery to ailments that I cannot recall. Acclimating to the spacious apartment was not difficult. We didn't have to ascend and descend three flights of stairs, and my father was able to arrive home earlier for supper.

Things were going well for my father, so he decided to pursue manufacturing. The building behind our apartment was owned by a candy distributor. After the owner passed away, his wife was unable to continue the business, so she sold the building to my father. The business flourished after he began manufacturing his own shoes. He gave each of us who were old enough an opportunity to earn an allowance by helping after school. Of course, he did not neglect the others who were too young: every Sunday we lined up to receive our share; it was comical to watch us at this time, seeing so many kids jumping up and down waiting to get paid. Dad was always in a good mood. I spent my money at the movies, and I also joined the Laurel and Hardy Club.

In 1938, my sister Thérèse was born at the new place, and my parents were happy. Eight children running around would drive anybody crazy, but not my father. He just worked harder and harder. When school was out, my brothers and sisters and I went off to the country for the summer to a place called Meulan-Hardricourt. This country town was about fifty kilometers northwest of Paris. The farm we stayed at belonged to a couple that my parents met through friends. We called the lady who took care of us Auntie Marthe. We saw her husband, Louie, only in the evenings. He never worked but arose very early in the morning to fish, never missing a day during the time I knew him. He had a cantankerous disposition. We had to take his lunch to him on time; otherwise, he would cuss us out.

I always thought Meulan-Hardricourt was a boring place; my parents' routine Sunday visits were the weekly highlights for me. I don't think the population exceeded 500. Days were spent running around in the fields, catching rabbits, picking fruit, and helping in the garden. The place we stayed had dirt floors and the bathroom was in the backyard: we simply dug a hole and put a bench over it. When it was full, we covered it and dug another hole. There wasn't much supervision, so along with David and Suzanne, my two older siblings, I was in charge of my younger siblings. Everyone else loved the outdoor play and adventure, but I was a city slicker; the country was not for me. Going back to school was always a breath of fresh air, but down the road, Meulan-Hardricourt would become the lifeline for most of us.

I became more involved in learning from and working with my father in his prospering business. His employees were a wealth of knowledge as well. I remember one in particular who was a leather cutter. At that time, everything was done by hand, so he taught me how to cut out patterns of leather for shoe taps. He would slip me a few francs on pay day.

We were happy and content with our lives. We would never have imagined that one man would soon shatter all that we knew and everything my father had worked so hard to accomplish.

Maurice Choroszez

Chapter 3

Veldrome D'Hiver

I graduated high school, and three of my brothers, Benjamin, Simon, and Joseph, and two of my sisters, Renée and Thérèse, went to Meulan-Hardricourt for summer vacation the week before Paris surrendered. I was reluctant in going, so my father allowed me to stay and help in the factory with my older brother David and my older sister Suzanne. Two days later, on June 14, 1940, the German Army marched into Paris. I stood on the street watching what was left of the French Army retreat in disarray. Many of them had lost their weapons in exchange for a bottle of wine in their hands.

The German Army was probably the most disciplined of any military force I had ever seen. They marched in parade, fresh and polite to everyone. Within a few days the French government capitulated, and France was another victim of Hitler. For a while after the occupation of Paris, life went on normally. Conflict was negligible, and the circulating rumors of abusive Nazi conduct seemed false.

My brother Jacques was born on August 27, 1940, increasing the family to nine children. Jews faced complications soon after with the Nazis forcing us to register at the police station. We were issued yellow Magen David stars to wear continually. Synagogues were shut down, and we were denied permission to attend movies, theaters, restaurants, or any public venues. Schools were off-limits as well. Jewish businesses of all kinds were mandated to display a sign in a window identifying it as such, dissuading public commerce. Walking the streets, inundated with fear of someone approaching unprovoked to beat me was a way of life. Fear of incarceration rendered us defenseless.

I was often afraid, removing my coat in public and carrying it under my arm. I did take chances a few times to see a movie. Only once did I run into an acquaintance. I fled the theater in a panic. I never divulged my conduct to my parents; they had enough fear. We did the best we could under the circumstances. We strictly worked and stayed inside as much as possible.

The status quo remained until 1941. I don't remember the month of the ominous night when Germans raided more than 100 Jewish homes, arresting several hundred Jews. My mother's cousin's husband, Abraham, was included. He was never heard from again. From that day forth we lived in perpetual fear, not knowing when the next raid would come. Friends of the family begged my father to seek refuge with his family, but I guess he could not believe that the Germans were tyrannically attempting to eliminate the Jewish population.

In May of 1942, my sister Fernande was born, growing our family to ten children. We thought my parents were immune to malady by virtue of their large family. Then it happened to us.

July 16, 1942, in the middle of the night, was the largest arrest en masse in the city of Paris. During the Veldrome d'Hiver roundup, the Germans pounded on the door and broke it down after we refused to open. Father, age thirty-eight; my sister Suzanne, age eighteen; my brother David, age seventeen, were arrested and taken to the police station. When the Germans and their sycophant, the French police, finished the following day more than 13,000 Jews had been arrested in all parts of the city. It was a plain and simple attempt to diminish the Jewish population in France. Families were broken with no second thoughts. They transferred the Jews to Drancy, a concentration camp located in the outskirts of Paris. They were never heard from again. My father and sister were on the same convoy, and my brother was separated from them. We learned much later that they perished at Auschwitz.

My mother, my new little sister, and I escaped the arrest. The French police only had orders to arrest Father, David, and Suzanne because they were foreign-born in Poland. The next day, my mother and sister joined my other brothers and sisters who were in hiding. My parents had decided to leave them in Hardricourt due to uncertainty over future security. I hid at a gentile-owned leather goods store that did business with my father. The owner had connections with the underground. Meanwhile, the SS pillaged our factory, shoe store, and apartment. They ripped off the wallpaper thinking we hid something behind. They went as far as removing the nails.

Right to left: Father, 36; David, 13; Bernard, 11

I was able to obtain false identification. I could not use the identification issued to me by the police department because it had the word JUIF (JEW) stamped on it. I then escaped to Lyon in Southern France a few days later. Life was miserable. I could not find a job, and I was nearly broke. I found others in the same situation. We collaborated and shared hotel rooms to cut expenses. The Germans continued raids as they were informed of our locale, so we were constantly on the move. I thought I could manage fending for myself, being the city slicker that I am, but my family was far.

I couldn't bear that lifestyle after a few months, so I retreated to Paris. I went to see a business friend of my father's and asked to sleep in the back of his place. He also owned a leather goods store, and since he wasn't Jewish, I felt safe there. Though I soon grew weary of sleeping on leather, and from the reports I received, the Germans had ceased from arresting Jews. So I got in touch with my mother by phone and told her I would be going back to the apartment.

After being in hiding about eighteen months from July 1942 to January 1944, she soon joined me with my little sister Fernande and my brother Ben—a gargantuan mistake. A few days later, again in the middle of the night, there was a pounding at the door. We would not open it. We knew what was happening. The Germans—aided by French police—broke the door to pieces. We didn't know who would be taken. A small closet concealed by wallpaper was too small for Benjamin, so I told him to get in bed under the covers, hoping they wouldn't see him, and instructed him to join the others if he was spared. Mother, Fernande, and I were arrested and incarcerated at the police station with hundreds of others. We stayed until dawn then were transported by bus to Drancy. We were neither fed before leaving nor upon arrival. Right off the buses, we went through a building and forfeited all valuables—all of our money and jewelry, everything was to be handed over (although we did manage to hide some things for sentimental reasons and in anticipation of needing something of value for the future). This was the beginning of the most miserable existence a person could live, but I was oblivious to my impending fate and that of my mother and little sister.

We were at Drancy for six days. During that time, we did nothing except try to keep the place clean with several hundred people contained in plain concrete buildings. We had very small beds and the place reeked of dirty bodies and excrement. All the boys and men had their heads shaved, and the women were given short haircuts. The food we were given was repugnant. Our last morning there, each person was dealt a loaf of bread with a hunk of salami and sent to the courtyard. Many buses were lined up to transport us. I managed to write a short letter and gave it to the bus driver when we boarded. It was addressed to my brother Ben. This was the last time he heard from me during my captivity. I gave the driver a gold pocket watch as tribute for delivering the letter. I learned after the war that he had, in fact, kept his word.

The buses took us to a railyard where we were lectured by German SS troops. They warned that if anyone escaped, others would be shot in reprisal. We were shoved into the cattle cars, packed to the point of immobility. Sitting or lying down was out of the question. They also placed a barrel of water in the car just before enclosing us and securing the door. When all the cars were packed and just before the doors were closed, a German officer repeated that if anyone escaped, a number of us would be shot in reprisal upon arrival to our destination. On a freezing winter Sunday morning our convoy left Paris with 1,500 people on board. We were about the one thousandth convoy to leave Paris for a place still unknown to the entire French population. At that time, it was perhaps the best-kept secret in the world.

Chapter 4

Auschwitz

We couldn't see where we were headed because the train car was padlocked—sixty men, women, and children per car. There was fighting, crying, and all kinds of hollering. We grew restless and tired. Some did try to sit or lay down, depriving enough space for others. We traveled like this for three days and three nights without seeing sunlight.

Those cattle cars were inhumane. We were without bathroom facilities or fresh air. The filth of people forced to relieve themselves in the unstopped train was unfathomable. The water lasted only the first day. The food consisted mainly of bread, and that too was gone by the second day. We were oblivious as to the duration of our journey, and many became vomitus and severely ill due to the intensely stressful conditions or old age. The day before we arrived, an old lady died. With bittersweet fortune, she was the lone casualty.

After the train stopped, we waited about two hours for the doors to be opened. We then understood our position a little more as roughly 100 SS troops and other inmates with large sticks and rubber hoses in hand awaited. We were hurried off the train; piercing cracks permeated the air as the heads and backs of those exiting too slowly were beaten. All the men were herded into a single line. More SS officers arrived, and then each of us, one at a time, had to walk in front of them. The women and children lined up to our right. The men were asked a few questions such as age and occupation. They examined us like livestock to determine who was potentially productive. We were then prompted to stay or move to the right line. By the end, I, along with approximately 250 people, was in the left line, and about 1,250 people were in the right line, including my mother and sister.

The SS were only interested in the more virile; the others were useless. The separation in front of the train ended and the line with the women, children, and some men too old to work were ushered away. We watched them head to a building that we soon learned was the gas chamber. My devoted, tender mother and my tiny, innocent sister were gassed and incinerated in the furnace, but I was callous, unable to shed any tears. I was sixteen when they died and unable to comprehend the veracity of the situation. A state of shock and uncertainty about the future was my reality.

My mother holding Fernande

Those of us fortunate enough to be in the left line were led in the opposite direction. We passed the station displaying the marquee our train passed under boasting in translation "Work makes you free" and discovered that we were in Auschwitz, Poland. Again, we had no idea that we had just landed at the largest of all concentration camps. People died daily in the gas chamber and crematorium. Auschwitz was later to become notorious as the camp where more than 1.5 million lives perished.

We arrived at the building where many other groups were led and made to strip nude and forcibly surrender the few possessions concealed since leaving Paris. Hiding anything at this point was impossible. Every orifice was checked from head to toe. I had managed to hide a gold ring that I bought myself several years back. It was tight on my finger, but when the SS noticed it, they told me to remove it. I pretended to be unable to take it off, hoping they would let me keep it, but before I had a chance to say anything, an SS grabbed my hand and ripped it off with a pair of pliers. Each person was given a complete shave from head to toe, without missing any part of our bodies. The concept of privacy and the fact that we were fellow human beings had vanished completely. We then had to enter a tank of disinfectant, then shower, and were immediately shoved outside in the nude, soaking wet and standing knee deep in snow. We had to wait until everyone finished, standing in the snow for what seemed to be the longest segment of recorded time. The SS then led us to a barracks and gave us two little rags. I started wiping myself, but then the SS in charge informed us that these were our socks. We received no undergarments, only a pair of blue and white striped trousers, a jacket, and a beret. The shoes were mismatched with wooden soles. We were dressed like criminals in a penitentiary.

We were then assigned to a barracks. I went directly to sleep, too exhausted to consider eating. Around 3:30 in the morning, a fellow inmate awoke us with a little bit of soup and a slice of black bread — our daily portion. This was the first time in a week we were given something warm to eat. The soup was rancid; I just could not force myself to stomach it; it was not fit for human consumption. Aside from water, the ingredients remain unknown. The experienced inmates in the barracks waited, knowing we wouldn't eat that garbage, having endured the same upon their arrival. As soon as we set down our bowls they swarmed in and ate. That was a pitiful sight. We couldn't understand the meaning of this until it happened to us. I lasted just beyond a week before giving in and eating the soup. It was either eat or starve, and by that time, whatever they gave us to eat was acceptable. We were taken after that first meal to another barracks not too far from ours to fill out some forms and answer some questions. Afterward, we herded through a line and received our lifetime serial number tattooed on our left forearm. From that day forth, I was known as prisoner number 173752. The process happened so quickly that I never saw the needle. I had been herded into a cattle car, given food unbefitting a pig, marched in front of soldiers like an animal for evaluation for slaughter, examined thoroughly in the most demeaning manner, and now stripped of my identity. We were never again called by name—just a number without a face.

After everybody was tattooed, we were relegated to our barracks for three weeks. We were only allowed to leave to perform detail work like cleaning the SS quarters and keeping their buildings clean. The work was easy, but hunger was setting in. The days were terribly long. I imagined Father's, Suzanne's, and David's fates to be similar; I attempted to find them, but the camp was too big to bear the task.

After about a month in the camp, a bunch of us were called to prepare for transfer to another camp. We were sent to Gleiwitz, Poland, where there was a coal mine. Thankfully, I was only there a couple of days and sent back to Auschwitz for an undisclosed reason. I suppose the transfer back was in my favor because the nature of the work in the coal mines was devastating; I was glad to be in Auschwitz where my opportunity for survival seemed to be more likely after witnessing what was happening to the poor souls working the mines. Very few survived, and those who did survive would have been better off dead.

The first day back I was assigned to a lousy detail called a commando. That commando entailed the heavy labor of fifty to seventy-five inmates. I had to carry large rocks weighing in excess of fifty pounds for the entire day without gloves or an overcoat. The ground and rocks were packed with ice and snow, and the temperature must have been around thirty degrees below zero. I cried like hell and wished for the first time that I were dead. The SS pushed us to work faster. My heart was about to rip apart. The pain was severe, but my endurance until the day's end was equally shocking. Upon our return to the barracks, I immediately proceeded to my bunk without eating any of that dirty water they called soup and saved my piece of bread for later. The exhaustion was unbearable.

The next day, I was assigned to a different commando, but it was no upgrade from the first. I had to shovel dirt for about sixteen hours without allowance of using the bathroom; getting something to drink or eat was out of the question. The ground was frozen, making digging next to impossible. My strength was leaving me unimaginably fast.

After work, I went to the barracks and ate some of the dirty soup. I made a habit of picking grass and dandelions to thicken the broth, which tasted better upon every occasion; starvation was overtaking me, and nutrition was taking on a new meaning. The following day, I was assigned to a new commando. This one had the reputation as best in Auschwitz. The work was not easy, but it was at least indoors where I could keep warm. We hauled building pipes—weighing more than we could individually handle—for underground construction. I was transferred to a new barracks where everyone in my new commando slept. Everyone was asleep when I arrived because transfers could only be made at night to avoid interfering with work. I didn't know what was to be expected with such a change.

The next evening, after another hard day's work, I received my daily ration. I remember being called by the barracks chief along with a few other inmates to the camp chief, who had a rubber hose in his hand and a little stool in front of him. Each of us was given fifteen lashes on the rear end. I was whipped for not fluffing the straw that I slept on. My buttocks were split and bleeding and my lungs were at capacity. How I wished to die! About two months elapsed before I could sit without pain.

I eventually learned a lot about how things ran in the concentration camp. Day after day we worked like slaves, anticipating the moment of death's deliverance. Many of my buddies around me died in unison. Some died of hunger, others from the strenuous work, and others from beatings and torture. The SS found pleasure in threatening and branding us with rubber hoses.

We were virtually cut off from the world. We never received any news or mail, though my Yiddish fluency served me well after some time, as I was able to pick up a lot of German conversation. This connected me a little more to the outside world as I overheard the guards' conversations. No one knew where we were.

We were like a bunch of animals rummaging garbage through cans and struggling for life. This was our life, day after day, never thinking of tomorrow. I just hoped to die and die fast to be put out of my misery. I had lost complete faith in God. As far as I was concerned, God did not exist. Many of the others prayed constantly. I berated them, exclaiming they were wasting their time. I told those praying that if their God answered them, to tell Him I was waiting for a piece of bread and to take my life quickly. Instead, these religious folk were dying quicker than the others. Maybe it was God's way of ending their misery. My time had not come, although I often considered taking my own life.

I attempted hanging myself, but in midst of sheer agony, the *will* to live interceded and spoke of a chance for survival, combined with the fear of death; I wanted to die but was afraid to die, so life continued despite my disbelief in God. I hoped my life would end soon. Those who couldn't keep up were sent to the gas chamber, only to be replaced by a new shipment. It was difficult making friends. I never knew how long one would live, so I resisted getting too close, rationalizing that loss would hurt less: any acquaintanceship was never regarded as friendship.

April Fool's Day, 1944, is a date I will never forget. We returned to our barracks from work and had just received our food rations when the bell rang for formation outside. We were all lined up in our commando's formation just like a parade, with a gallows erected before us. Several SS officers with machine guns stood on either side of the gallows. We were ignorant of what was to take place until one of our fellow inmates was brought out of the jail and led up to the gallows. An SS officer then read to us why this man was to be hanged as a lesson to us—a bit different from school lectures. The man attempted escape and that in and of itself was a major, unpardonable crime. How the inmate attempted escape remained unknown: the camp was completely surrounded by a double row of electric wires with SS posted between the two rows and German Shepherds every so many feet along with sentries brandishing machine guns.

Escape was impossible. We stood in silence watching the body drop and flail in agony until he turned blue. We then had to march past and salute the SS officers standing next to the gallows. We returned to the barracks, but I could not eat my filthy soup and just laid it on my bed. That was the first hanging I'd ever witnessed. Thinking about it was nauseating. I dreamt about it all night.

The days and time dragged on as the work intensified. I was constantly hungry and consumed with finding food. The sensation is likened to being kicked in the stomach and heaving. My weight had dropped dramatically, and I soon developed a fever with the chills. I did not inform anyone out of fear of being gassed and ending up like the others.

I worked my job a few more days, and in extreme weakness, I could no longer stand. I climbed the scaffolding of the work site to lie down on the roof for a while. I don't know how long I was sleeping but was finally awoken by someone ordering me to report to the kapo—a prisoner in charge of the barracks or appointed as squadron chief. Some were nice; others were murderers, defectors, homosexuals. I reported, and he stated that some SS officers found me asleep during an inspection. They filed a report, so disciplinary action had to be taken. I was lashed ten times on the rear and transferred that same evening to another commando. I was seventeen years old, but I cried like a baby, not only due to the pain from the beating, but also because I knew it would be tougher. I sat in the barracks until bedtime, waiting for someone to apprehend me, but nothing happened, so I went to sleep. I was awakened around 10:00pm by the barracks chief who brought me to my new commando. This commando only contained youth between the ages of fifteen and eighteen. I was hopeful that this would be much easier: I couldn't imagine children enduring hard labor.

I looked around the next morning to speak with someone. Not everyone in the barracks was from the same country. I eventually found two from France. We were the only Frenchmen among 250 Hungarians and 5 Dutchmen. The barracks chief was a young Communist German sentenced to a concentration camp since 1933 when Hitler came to power. Shortly after Hitler became Chancellor, any German at odds with him, regardless of political affiliation, was arrested and sent to a concentration camp. I asked about the nature of the work we were obligated to and was told that our commando was assigned to a different job daily depending on need.

We went right to work that morning, and my new kapo asked about the stipulations of my transfer. We didn't exactly hit it off; he was not an appealing fellow. Actually, he was a murderer convicted of killing his wife and daughter and given a life sentence. When Auschwitz opened, he was assigned there not as a criminal but as a big wheel. The first day in this new commando, I worked like a horse, carrying big tanks filled with oxygen to a building under construction. We worked all day without rest, and we were not permitted to use the bathroom without consent. If we moved too slowly, we were whipped. The SS had their laughs during this daily routine. I never found an SS guard with even a little understanding of the fact that we were all human beings, regardless of religious difference.

In the afternoon, I was finally allowed to use the restroom—a hole in the ground covered by a board. There were about fifteen other fellows tired and recuperating. I don't know how long we were there, but the kapo stormed in shouting and swinging his rubber hose, striking me on the back and forcing me to the ground relentlessly until I grabbed a rock and struck him in the face. Fortunately, he was a kapo and not an SS, or else I would have been shot on the spot. He beat me over the head and back in escalated fury until I fell unconscious. I awoke saturated with blood from a large laceration running from behind my ear to my mouth; my two buddies had to carry me back to the barracks that evening. I was afraid to go on sick call that night and thought it better to wait until morning. I ate some of my soup and went right to bed. The pain was too severe to fall asleep, though. It was simply an endless night.

I was the first one up in the morning and went straight to complain about my injuries. I don't know what compelled me to report it and go on sick call because doing so was a potential death sentence. I suppose I just wanted it to be over. I didn't care if I lived or died; I believed there was something better than this hell. I went to see the barracks chief and told him everything that happened at work. He told me not to go that day; rather, he would place me on sick call. I didn't know there was such a thing as a hospital for inmates. I figured they would send me to the gas chamber, but I guess since I was still able to work, they didn't want to finish me off yet. After all the commandos left for work, he took me to the hospital. The doctor took my temperature and said I had a high fever. He patched up my face and gave me a slip of paper excusing me from work that day, but this did not help; I was still put to work. Since all the other commandos had left, I was assigned to clean up the camp for the day. I didn't mind too much; it was the easiest day I'd had in a long time. I only did what was necessary and nothing more, slacking off as often as possible. Later in the afternoon, I snuck back to the barracks to lie down for a while but could not fall asleep; the pain was too intense, and I shivered exorbitantly. At around five o'clock my fever grew worse, and I found myself back on sick call. Again, the doctor put something on my face and told me to return the next morning.

Because I was a hard worker and did not complain to anyone regarding my illness, I was a commodity, so they kept me around. The kapo was responsible for reporting to the SS, so clandestine activity was possible. The SS did not keep track of daily operations. They would occasionally perform night visits to barracks to test the virility of the inmates by having us run around the barracks. Those who were unable to keep up with the physical demands were removed from the group to be gassed and incinerated the next morning. A kapo showing preferential treatment apart from SS discretion was always risking his health. I was simply fortunate with favorable circumstances.

Chapter 5

Aside from the Obvious

The next morning, May 27, 1944, I went back on sick call and was admitted to the hospital. I was certain my life would end. I could not fathom the SS wasting the doctor's time on me since they never had with others. It was just a matter of time until I would be sent to the gas chamber with a few other guys who were there. However, once again, by some miracle, my time was extended. Instead, they took my dirty clothes away and told me to shower and go to bed. Before noon, the doctor came to take my temperature. My fever was very high but without a clear diagnosis. Without considering that the fever was caused by the infection from the wound on my face, the doctor merely prescribed ice packs to break the fever.

The ice packs did nothing the first day. The fever just burnt all over. The doctor saw me the next day and still could not figure out what ailed me. He finally said that the fever was caused by an infection that would have to heal by itself. Everything remained about the same the following day. While the doctor examined me, a fellow walked by and peered in, calling me by name. This was the first time in several months someone had called me by my name. It took a while before I recognized my friend Maurice Wax. He lived two blocks from me in Paris. I was thrilled to see him; I constantly wondered what had befallen him. He was arrested about a month and a half before me for failing to register for work in Germany. His emaciated body resembled a skeleton more than a live human being. All we could utter at first was how the world was such a small place, meeting again several thousand kilometers from home among the survivors. Despite the horrors of our current status, we just could not stop talking about the good old days and wondered if we would ever see home again. Maurice died shortly thereafter, just lacking the strength to survive; he gave up the will to live.

The time passed quickly apart from my awareness. Not until the doctor returned did I realize it was late afternoon. He gave me something to eat, but the food would not go down my throat. He prescribed ice bags for my stomach without my understanding. I remained in the same condition for another week. Then one morning, the doctor came in with another doctor—an inmate who was an ear, nose, and throat specialist. He looked at my face and knew right away what was wrong. My right ear was cut inside and so infected that he immediately cared for it, saving my hearing. I don't know exactly what he did because he administered a shot of anesthesia. I started feeling much better that evening. I slept well until about 5:00am when another buddy woke me up. I didn't know if he was smiling or crying, but he was so blissful that it took me a while to understand why. He had overheard the doctors talking about the Americans landing in Normandy. I didn't believe it until someone passed our window and corroborated the good news. That day, we really thought we had a chance to live in freedom again someday, but that was only a dream for the time being.

In the meantime, my face was not healing. The doctor led me to a room and had me lie down on a table. He instructed me to start counting, and then put a mask on my face. All I can remember was counting to twenty-one and waking to my face wrapped with white paper bandages. The doctor told me that he had to open the cut on my face to clean out the infection. I didn't feel anything; I was floating in the air.

My health wasn't any better the next day. I still had a high fever with fatigue and cranial pain too severe to permit sleep. Another week passed in this same condition. I could not eat anything, and if it was even possible, I grew even weaker. I asked someone to retrieve my buddy. When he came, I told him "this will be my last night alive." I asked him to find my family and inform them of what happened to me if he ever got out alive. After midnight, I was delirious and unaware of my surroundings. My buddy sought the doctor, who injected me with something. It was miraculous that this was French doctor, who was able to cover up my presence in the hospital. If the SS knew about me, I may have been sent to the crematorium.

The fever dropped a bit the next day, but I hung between life and death. For the following ten days my condition remained the same, and then I started to recover. The fever dropped, and on the final day of June, the doctor informed me that I was to be discharged from the hospital the next day. I implored him to request my transfer to another commando because the previous was deleterious. He did so successfully. The next morning, I was released from the hospital and went straight to work. I was no longer sick but pallid from being bedridden. The new commando was huge and not much better than the former. The first day at work was very demanding, and I cried with no one to confide in. We were unloading trains containing all sorts of smashed metal and steel pieces. The scrap metal was to be used for the German Army. We were refused rest the entire day. The kapo was a dirty guy who watched us intently.

After we got back to camp that evening, I went to the doctor and asked to work in the camp for a few days. With extreme fortune I worked five days in the camp doing some detail work. The five days were easy; I wished every day to be the same. I returned to the commando the sixth day. The days passed at a snail's pace. The work intensified as I lost even more strength. We were constantly hit by the kapo. He always complained that we were not working fast enough. Not one day were we spared from beatings on the back. My skin was broken and bloody. We were powerless to prevent the beatings.

Chapter 6

Unfit and Irrelevant

One night after eating dirty soup and falling asleep, we were awakened around 1:00am by SS officers. They made us take off our clothes, then walk, then run single file inside the barracks before the SS officers. A few of the weakest were weaned out, deemed unfit for work and irrelevant to life. These poor souls were handpicked for the gas chamber and exterminated the next day. After that night, the process was repeated often. Those remaining were given a shot in the heart. I have never learned of the nature of that experiment. We learned the next day going to work that the same thing happened in all the barracks. Hundreds potentially were weeded out every three or four weeks.

Nothing changed until August 20, 1944. It was a Sunday morning and only a few commandos went to work, including mine. We worked until ten o'clock when the sirens sounded three times for the first time in my hearing since entering the camp. We surveyed the area and saw a few civilians and SS troops run away. We were left alone and relieved. We sat down for a while then saw a formation of airplanes flying directly over-head. Bombs suddenly fell, enveloping the surrounding terrain. No more than a few seconds were needed to find a hole for cover. Some guys just stood aghast, watching the whole thing. A bomb fell near us, blowing up some large pipes. Railroad tracks were decimated. Some bombs detonated right on top of the hole we were in, sealing us in the hole. Two hours after the sirens blared, some commandos came to dig us out. We were trapped about five hours. The devastation and carnage was evident. Many buildings were demolished. Many men lay motionless with death. The big chimney was still up; this was the target, but they missed. This chimney and the buildings around it was the command center.

We had no rest for three days and all were solicited to repair the roads. We didn't have anything to eat because the water pipes broke, so the soup could not be made. The SS told us that trucks were unable to enter the camp, so we couldn't eat. During that time many men died from arduous labor and starvation. A few days were required for water lines to be restored. Work was strenuous: two days we worked to fix the road, pipe lines, and damaged buildings

On September 13, the sirens blew again after the initial damage was nearly repaired. Most started running, but I first looked at the sky. Planes soared in bombardment. I ran for shelter but witnessed everything. The bombs were on target this time. We were ecstatic, thinking maybe the SS men would abdicate and quit building, but this was foreign to German reputation. We were again forced to rebuild regardless of ensuing deaths. Food was lacking but work abounded. We didn't mind this; we hoped the planes would hit the chimney. Food was nonexistent for about a week until the water pipes were repaired. We had to fix the roads again.

We worked like hell days after the bombing. My stomach ached with hunger. I couldn't work anymore, so I looked around and saw the kapo working with some other fellows. I took off from work and went to the civilian mess hall in search of anything to eat. Nobody was there, so I went in and took a bowl of soup. I didn't get to taste any of it because the chief of police of the camp took it away from me. He recorded my serial number and let me go. I was sicker than ever with terror of something ill befalling me.

One week later, we returned from work and stood in formation to witness three men hanged from the gallows. They were caught by the SS attempting to steal food. Before returning to our barracks, the barracks chief told me to report to the SS orderly room. I went there immediately to get it over with. There were some other guys with me, eight all together for the same reason. We didn't wait too long before an SS sergeant came in and read our serial numbers. He told us that we should all be hanged for attempted larceny; instead, each was to receive twenty-five lashes on the back. A fellow, about thirty years of age, was the first. I erroneously said to myself, "This isn't as bad as I expected." They started whipping that fellow, and at the fifth lash he started crying and rolled over, but the SS men didn't care. He was lashed five more times then went limp. He died shortly thereafter. I was the fourth guy to receive punishment. I didn't cry, but after receiving a few lashes, my lungs felt like they exploded. I fell unconscious until the next morning. My back was completely raw and bloody; I remembered nothing more about the event. I found out that morning that only two of the eight remained alive. I pondered the probability of being one of the two. I worked that same morning. The barracks chief told me not to go on sick call or else they would dispose of me.

For one week, I labored with unbearable pain. This new infection lasted about a month. I was then called one morning with some other fellows and transferred without notice to another commando. This one was worse than the prior. We had to carry sacks of cement from railroad cars up to the fifth floor of a building under construction. The SS guards watched us like hawks.

Meanwhile, the planes returned often; though many times they simply flew over without bombing. The SS were more afraid than we were. The status quo remained until a few days before Christmas. Everybody spoke of good times at home before the war. A rumor circulated the camp that we would receive a double ration of soup for the holidays and maybe some bread. But I didn't expect anything since I knew something would arise to spoil it even if it was true, and I was right.

The Russian military commenced a major offensive. The day before Christmas, planes returned, bombarding the camp and hitting their target with precision. The damage was so extensive that the SS decided to discontinue the labor, which of course did not anger us. We didn't have anything to eat on Christmas day, but this was overshadowed by the visible disgust on the faces of the SS officers losing faith in their leaders. A couple of days later, we started rebuilding the place. No progress was made because the planes returned at least twice a day for about a week. The SS began shipping out some of their men and equipment. Further rumors circulated about the German army's poor condition and potential loss of the war. The Germans were celebrating New Year's Day, 1945; it passed like any other day, but we had more hope than ever before because the sound of Russian artillery was near.

Our work was temporarily halted, so we knew something was happening. The SS were visibly angry; they could not believe their army being pushed back and possibly losing the war. By now, we were constantly on alert with nobody in sight to manage us. The SS hid in their shelters. Many of us contemplated escape but lacked clothing and knew vast distance could not be trekked without our uniform and due to weakness. The days were eons, but by January 10 the SS didn't know what to do with us as they waited for orders from Berlin. They speculated that the Russian

Army could be stopped, but we heard they were close to us and moving faster than expected. We figured freedom was within five days. We waited and waited, however, in vain. The artillery fire drew closer and the sky looked like it was on fire. On January 18, we were overjoyed to learn that the Russian Army was only twelve kilometers away. Everyone sang, but the bell rang for a formation that same evening at 4:30. We had to fall in within minutes. We were informed by the SS that all were to be evacuated; none were to remain behind. Those unable to persevere would be disposed of. That meant shot.

At exactly 5:00pm the entire camp left for Gleiwitz and other destinations about fifty kilometers from Auschwitz. It was dark and freezing— maybe thirty or forty degrees below zero. The snow surpassed our knees. We didn't have anything to carry, so the SS guardsmen gave us their luggage to haul on our backs. After a few hours on the road, we met other fellows from surrounding camps. We rested for about ten minutes then walked again, but with the camps together. There were about 100,000 men in a line stretching for many kilometers with SS alongside toting machine guns. We journeyed a substantial distance by midnight in worsening weather. My feet were frozen within the sodden wooden shoes. I cannot grasp how we were able to walk as we hoisted our legs out of the overlapping snow with each step. Many men stalled. Those who fell were shot on the spot by the clean-up SS commando. They had orders that none should be left behind alive; the machine guns went off all night. Thousands upon thousands died for lack of tenacity. Those poor guys fought for life, hoping to be free someday. They died like flies. I walked unconsciously like a man who just left the nut house; my mind was numbed to incoherency.

A little Frenchman—a mutual aide during the journey—jolted my senses. I glanced at the SS walking beside me. His tongue hung like a dog's as he muttered complaints. He was without lack but was entrapped like us. There was no transportation even for ailing SS officers. He didn't get too far. Blood drained from his nose and mouth as he tried to walk a little farther, but he collapsed to the ground. Another SS came from behind and shot him in the head. I was emboldened and encouraged to continue walking, knowing that what happened to us also happened to them. We walked until daylight dawned at seven o'clock. We stopped in a small village to rest, not on our behalf, but for fatigued SS men. They worked all night, guarding and killing those who fell. Everyone lay down on the road; I slept until noon. We then continued. Approximately 30,000 men were missing. Most were killed; a few managed to escape. I walked a few kilometers and was at the end of my rope. My legs no longer supported me. I was sick with starvation. I looked at my buddy next to me, who was as stoic as when we had left camp. During the first twenty kilometers he didn't say a word as though trained specifically for the task. I told him, "I can't go." He didn't say a word. He just grabbed my arm and dragged me most of the way to Gleiwitz.

It was 7:00pm on January 19 when we entered the camp. It was just big enough for about 2,000 men;

we numbered close to 60,000. The first to arrive had a place to sleep in one of the six barracks. Since I was one of the last in, I had to settle for sleeping in the snow with the others. I don't remember falling asleep and didn't wake up until much later the next day. There was no mention of food because none was available—the third straight day without any. It was a miracle that so many remained. A formation was ordered that afternoon to count the remaining prisoners. Only a little over 20,000 were alive. Some may have escaped. The premises were littered with dead bodies. The place looked more like a cemetery than a camp. I'm not sure what happened the next two days because I slept.

We had to make a single line and walk in front of a few SS officers. They inspected each of us and commanded us to either the left or the right line. We knew instantly what was about to happen. I was sent to the left between two barracks without knowing the locale of the guys in the right. It took only a few minutes to realize they were the ones who could still work and were to be spared. It didn't matter to me anymore; I just about had enough. I was frail; standing was an enormous task, so I lay down and fell asleep.

A couple hours later, we were awakened by the sound of gunfire. The SS surrounded the two barracks and targeted us. I thought my last day in the world had finally come. Death was entirely appealing as a result of chronic fatigue and starvation. Bodies toppled en masse. Many shielded themselves with the life-less corpses of others. Blood saturated the ground. I crawled to a nearby corner and hid under the deceased for protection from the streaking bullets. I suddenly felt something graze my forehead, and then another bullet hit me in the back. It apparently first hit some-one lying on top of me and only slightly penetrated my back. I attempted to survey my surroundings but only noticed blood streaming down my face. I was afraid to move, knowing the SS were watching for live bodies. The pile of men saved me. Many remained alive; some were smart enough to fall immediately when the shooting commenced. A few of the living were in poor shape with bullets in their bodies and significant blood loss. We lay there until midnight covered us with darkness, then we crawled one by one to join those who were earlier spared.

Chapter 7

Buchenwald

Early the next morning, a train of open-top cattle cars arrived. The SS gave the order to board. The group was numerous, so they didn't bother checking us. Approximately 10,000 decrepit souls were shipped 160 per car that day. We waited in the cars until that evening, and then the train started moving to an unknown destination. Many of us were so close to deliverance, with death so near, but at least our survival was plausible. We knew the Germans were losing the war, but this had to be ignored for the time being to maintain vigilance.

After leaving Poland, the train traveled along the Czechoslovakian border. Fights broke out among us the first day. We took turns sitting to rest due to over-crowding, and eating — as usual — was out of the question. We slept on top of one another that night, and while awake, we fought. Our faces were swollen in the morning from being kicked all night. I don't know how many times I was kicked, but my old wounds hemorrhaged and blood streaked my face.

The second day was worse: hunger had set in to the point of inducing savagery. Fights were more frequent. A few of the men died, so we just dumped their bodies from the train to provide more space. Just before nightfall, the train stopped for a couple of hours. I was famished and told my buddy I was going to jump off the train to eat some snow. Before I had a chance, he jumped and gathered up some snow but didn't have a chance to raise it to his mouth. An SS guard saw him and shot him down like a dog. My eyes popped from their sockets at the sight of his blood staining the white snow. I was dazed. I couldn't believe that such a nice guy now lay dead. He saved my life a couple of times and now I witnessed his blood emitting from his nose and mouth. This was asinine. I lost my appetite, completely forgetting my demand for food.

The train started chugging, and we left behind several dead. I beheld a mini cemetery. The fighting intensified with killing for survival. We had a little more room to lie down and sleep. A body was tossed from the train with each death. By the third morning through Czechoslovakia, the car was nearly empty and a few of the dead still had to be discarded. We watched folks venture to work as we came upon a bridge, and people threw food into our car. We fought for each morsel all for naught: as each tried to grab a portion, the food was squandered by our selfish insistence, squashing and crumbling what was given. More than ten men lost their lives during that struggle. A boy and his father fought each other; the son tried to kill his father with a wooden shoe. The father was able to gather a few crumbs of bread, but he would not share them with his son. The father's head was gashed open with blood seeping downward, but he did not

hesitate to remove his shoe and beat his son unconscious. They both died.

The typical person cannot comprehend what
happened. Food was more precious than life. We
were worse than savages, but looking back, I am not
shocked at how callous we had become—throwing
dead people off the train with no regard, fighting over
crumbs. It was the place our brains and bodies had to
go for survival. Our destiny was no longer ours.

The train stopped on the night of January 26. The
doors of the train were opened, and we were ordered
to exit. I was weak and had trouble walking, but the
first thing I did was fall on the snow to eat as much
possible. A little while later we fell into formation.
The number missing from the convoy was inconceivable. In just a short time, so many lives, bodies, were
absent forever. We walked a few kilometers to a camp
with the sign "Buchenwald" located near the city
of Weimar, Germany. It was known as the camp of
death. We didn't know who called it that because we
thought nothing could be worse than Auschwitz, but

this concentration camp was the largest in Germany, founded in 1933 soon after Hitler came into power.

We entered the camp and were contained in a small area encompassed with barbed wire. We stayed there until an SS officer came out and directed us into a building one at a time. Upon entering the building, our clothes were taken from us. Naked and in a single line, we passed in front of a fellow administering injections in the heart. This was the same shot we received every three to four weeks by Dr. Mengele. We never found out what it was, but I assume it was probably experimental. Then we walked by another SS inspecting our orifices for smuggled objects. Afterward, we were given haircuts and our bodies were shaved from head to toe. We then entered a small swimming pool filled with disinfectant to eliminate the filth accumulated during our trip. We took a shower but did not have anything to dry off with, so we stayed in the shower room. One man's patience finally expired, so he opened a door to an adjacent room. We stood petrified; inside the room were mounds of dead bodies.

We wondered why they would trouble themselves with cleaning us to just kill us in the gas chamber. Apparently, they needed us for something, or else they would not have spared our lives. When everyone was finished, they marched us through an underground tunnel to another building, where we were given some clothes. Then they took us to a barracks big enough for 200 men. We numbered about 1,800. There were no beds; we fought for a little space just to lie down. I fought for life that night to preserve a little corner that I claimed.

The Germans selected a few men the next day to build some shelters on each side of the walls. Each shelter was supposed to hold four men, but we were fortunate to get nine into each. That afternoon we were called into formation and told to form a single line into the barracks. A kapo at the door gave each of us a small piece of black bread and a little bit of soup in a dirty helmet. I didn't eat mine right away; it was the first food I had seen in eight days. I was afraid to eat. I wanted to keep it forever, but I realized what I was holding and devoured it, left wanting more.

The next morning, we were called for work—carrying rocks all day, covering up an underground shelter built for the commanding officers of the camp and their families in case of an air raid. We lacked water to wash ourselves. They had just enough to make the little soup we were served. We slept with our clothes for fear of being robbed during the night. We had to watch those next to us. We were no longer allies; it was every man for himself.

One morning, instead of work, everyone was called outside and taken to a building to fill out a form. An SS officer then asked if a welder was among us. Naturally, in the hopes of avoiding a day of hard labor, most answered affirmatively, including me. We spent the entire day in formation, waiting for everyone to be interviewed. We then returned to the barracks to receive our soup and bread. We were waiting to hear from the SS about the welder they were looking for, but nothing came of it. The days were long, and we still waited for a miracle. We knew the American Army was not far away.

Meanwhile, many of the guys were mysteriously dying; dysentery and typhus were claiming them along with starvation. Those bodies were removed, providing a little more room in the barracks.

We were outside one morning as I spoke with a man from southern France. He was married with two children. He shared with me his plans about his life upon returning home. Then, suddenly, while he was speaking to me, he literally dropped dead. I could not believe a person could die so fast. One moment this guy had a joyful dream of someday reuniting with his family, but dysentery claimed him as well. He wasn't dead for but a few minutes when others jumped him and looted his clothes. After that, I believed my day to die was fast approaching, but I still hoped liberation would come first.

A few days later at dawn, we were inspected by the SS for cleanliness then given an injection in the heart like the one upon arrival to the camp. (For years, I sought to learn the exact nature of the injected substance, but was repeatedly told it was impossible know.) I was one of the first to receive the shot then waited for the others as a big wheel strolled by, carrying a box filled with bread. I didn't know what possessed me, but I followed him. While there was some pushing, I managed to steal a half loaf of bread. The person checking the cart was oblivious, but the guy who was in the rack saw and jumped me, trying to seize the bread from me. I told him to shut up and I would give him half; however, he coveted the entire half loaf. We fought, catching the attention of the other prisoners. The person carrying the bread box realized some was missing. He approached us and caught me red-handed. He snatched it away and hit me—knocking me out cold—and then presumably called the barracks chief. I was punished by having to do extra detail without food all day.

As I worked the following day, I found some potato peels. I didn't tell anybody and ate as much as possible. They were covered with dirt yet appetizing. We quit work early that afternoon and returned to the barracks. They called off a bunch of numbers, and then 600 men were shipped out a couple of hours later. Turnover was rapid. I watched yearlong acquaintances depart in an instant. I was soon the only one left from the group. I wanted to cry terribly, but the tears stalled.

An alert came during work the day after, so the SS imposed early retirement from work to camp. We heard planes soaring and bombs falling. The city of Weimar was the target, only a few miles away. The men transported the day before were on a train caught in the bombing. The survivors were returned to camp. That same evening, the SS took about 100 of the strongest men to town to help civilians clean up and salvage damaged goods, a timely fortune for those able to gather anything for food. They brought some food back for themselves, and themselves only—it wasn't all for one and one for all, but rather one for one and none for all. We no longer worked on account of repeated alerts. They sometimes lasted half a day.

To say we looked like degenerate bums would be generous. Our clothes were tattered and torn; we were dirty, stinking of something awful. We lay down and didn't care to get up for the filthy soup. We were too weak to use the restroom, continually sensing our last hour swiftly approaching.

My eighteenth birthday came and went as we remained in that condition until March of 1945, wondering what preserved us from looming death. There was hardly any food and more dirt than we could bear. Men from other evacuated camps were relocated to Buchenwald as the Allies encroached. Then, about the fifth of March in the middle of the night, they woke us up for relocation. Without any notice, we were on the road walking to the train. More than 500 of us herded into the cattle cars. We had enough cars for the SS to put seventy men and twenty-two troopers in each car. For the first time we had some room to lie down. A little while later, the train started toward yet another unknown destination. Morale was low — expecting freedom from the enclosing American Army, yet again at the last moment the SS exported us elsewhere.

Chapter 8

Holzen

The first day was boisterous with men fighting amongst themselves. The SS did nothing. I guess they thought their job was made easier if we killed each other. We received no rations as the dirty Nazis ate their lunch in front of us, provoking us to jealousy. We just sat gazing with our eyes as big as apples, as a dog begs for food, but, as usual, they were delighted to witness our suffering. That night was noisier than usual; we found out why in the morning. All of the SS supply of food and drinks was stolen. The SS troopers beat us ferociously with large leather belts. Things progressively worsened thereafter. Whenever a noise was made, the SS beat us more. We strove for silence, but someone always wanted more room, resulting in conflict. After three days and nights of travel, we arrived in Holzen. We walked through town to reach the camp with our hands over our faces in protection from German townsmen hurling garbage at us and children throwing rocks and spitting at us. We eventually reached the camp at the top of a hill. It was small with a maximum occupancy of 800 men; we totaled 1,100 men. The camp lacked decent facilities. Water for drinking and soup making was supplied by a small river near the camp. An easier life was expected at this camp, considering the need for temporary laborers for big jobs; however, next morning's work proved otherwise.

About forty men formed a commando. They took us up into the mountains about ten kilometers from camp. We hauled massive logs all the way back to camp. What should have been a twelve-man task was instead a three-man haul under Nazi oversight. The walk was grueling as we staggered and fell with the logs on our backs, but the SS perfunctorily beat us as motivation to move faster. Extraordinary tenacity and courage enabled us to complete the task. The source of tenacity and strength necessary to accomplish the task is impossible to explain. Someone of obscure identity had to be watching over me — almost a reflexive thought. There was simply an innate sense that this was true despite my professed beliefs.

Our curiosity about their plans for the wood was answered upon returning to camp when we took the logs to where some other men were whittling them down into small pieces. I talked to one of the men who said we had to haul the logs in every day for heating the SS barracks and cooking because coal was scarce. I worked this job all day until 5:00pm at roll call. Thirty minutes later, they distributed our soup, but I was too exhausted to wait for my serving; I had lain down instead and fell asleep.

Suicide was attractive that following morning when possible torture by the SS troopers was pending, but something continued to motivate me, feeding me thoughts of better days to come. They put me in another formation, and we walked more than fifteen kilometers. We again had to venture through town: kids in Nazi uniforms, women, and others threw rocks and other objects at us. After almost two hours of brisk walking, we came to a vast subterranean establishment. We were all assigned a job: some carried rocks and some dug. I was given an air hammer and told to break up rocks. I worked all day without rest as the SS watched us vigilantly. We didn't stop until nightfall, and then we had to march back to camp.

I worked this job for about a week until the night I caved in. I could not go on any longer. I went on sick call and cried like a baby in front of the doctor. He gave me a slip to stay in camp for three days to do some light work, but I wished that I never went on sick call. I worked hard in the camp. I had to carry rocks all day around the house of the camp's SS commander. He incessantly watched us with his dog beside him. One man fell and could not get up, so the SS commander set his dog on him. The dog chewed his clothes off and bit him all over his body.

He helplessly lay on the ground bleeding and died a few hours later.

After three days, I went to work digging miles and miles of ditches for underground cable. This was better than the other job. Our SS guard was a young man who was 100 percent Nazi. He did nothing short of deifying Hitler in his speech. He walked around with a stick in hand, and every time he spotted me stopped for any reason—like wiping my face—he would hit me on the head and beat me into an unconscious stupor. One day he hit me with the butt of a rifle on my neck, busting the rifle in two. He was livid because he had to report how it ended up in that condition, so because of that, he kicked me in the groin. I fell down and was left that way.

I worked that job for ten days. One morning after roll call, we did not work. The American Army was not far. We were reinvigorated to fight for life. We returned to the barracks, and I had lain down to rest. However, a short while later the guy who slept next to me woke me up saying that he heard we were being evacuated that day. The Nazis were in a state of shock. They were running left and right unconcerned with the prisoners. We went to the kitchen where the soup was made and ate all we wanted. The soup had been made the day before, and was sour like a lemon, but I didn't care. It was more wondrous than the delicacies of France.

We had a formation at noon and were told we would be leaving in a couple of hours. The two hours seemed like a day. I was outside sitting down next to a kapo and some other guys listening in on their conversation indicating that no roll call would be taken as we departed. I saw an opportunity to hide. I informed a buddy of what I had heard, and we decided to stick together and try. When the time came, we waited to be the last ones in the barracks and hid ourselves in the attic instead of going outside. There was just enough room to lie down. Just as the formation outside was ready to leave, a few SS officers entered the barracks in search of anyone hiding. We held our breath, and in a short time they left. We stayed in our place a little while longer then heard a noise. Two fellows trying to escape climbed into our same attic, erupting in an altercation over the limited space. The commotion attracted the SS left behind for cleanup. They beat the hell out of us, killed one of the fellows, and badly injured my buddy. I had to carry him outside to join the others. We were taken to the railroad station where we had previously arrived. While we ventured through town, citizens lauded our departure, spitting and heaving garbage at us.

Chapter 9

En Route to Hamburg: Bergen-Belsen

The train rolled as soon as we boarded. The rumor was that we were headed for Hamburg and from there would sail to an island. We traveled for two long days without food, but had acclimated by then. Nothing changed; every departure was the same. We stopped at a small camp, but no one knew what to do with us. They didn't have any room, so the SS in charge of our transport was told by the commanding officer of the camp to continue onward. We again departed, and a day and a half later, we came to an underground camp. Over the camp was a strategic railroad station. It was very dangerous to remain there; the Allied Air Force came often; nevertheless, we stayed overnight. The following morning, some inmates from that camp were loaded onto the train with us. We numbered about 3,300 with 140 per car, just enough room to stand. We stood there a couple of hours, then something humorous dawned on us: a whole bunch of women were in the cars adjacent to ours—the first we had seen in a year.

We were off to Hamburg, hearing the women cry that first night. For some reason the men fought as a result. The train was moving very slowly in response to numerous alerts. The roar of the planes was near. The SS stopped the train, posting guards all around to prevent escape. We had been riding for three days.

Then on April 1, the train stopped for an alert. We saw planes, small like birds in the sky. Right away, the SS organized themselves around us, armed with machine guns. We watched the planes swoop down and bomb the factories. Fire soared into the air as the explosives decimated the buildings. The train then took off, but we stopped a few miles later at the

Celle railroad station. We were surprised to hear that we would be eating soon. Once again, the SS posted themselves around the train with their machine guns. They opened the last car and retrieved the food. By now, we had almost forgotten what the word food meant, being without for eight days. The distribution was too slow; we could hardly wait. However, any hope for a morsel dissipated with alert sirens blaring yet again as the Royal Air Force approached. This, of course, caused an immediate disruption of food distribution. We were merely two cars from our turn when the alert sounded. The bombers were directly overhead; regardless, we were sure they would not drop bombs on us. It was inconceivable that our allies could make such a mistake given our visibility. Our attire was clearly the common prisoner's under Nazi authority. Even among the weary, a little wit followed as someone remarked, "Hey buddies, if you are going to drop some bombs, at least wait until we've had our food served and our bellies are full." I would have liked to laugh at his joke, but suddenly without warning, the RAF dropped bombs right on top of us. We all ducked for cover laying on top of one another for protection. My thoughts were of my mother. For the first time in years I prayed a few words, despite my loss of faith in God. Knowing that my mother had died in the gas chamber, I prayed, "Mom, I guess I won't see you anymore, I turned to God." Then bombs fell all around like the rains of India, with ear-splitting explosions.

After the first bombing ceased, I sensed a burning sensation on my back. I looked back and saw that the car directly behind us, as well as the rear section of our car had been completely reduced to rubble. The car in front received similar treatment. The scene was unsightly; many men had dismembered limbs and ran or crawled in a wild frenzy seeking aid in vain. Through a miracle alone, I was not injured. However, my buddy was not as fortunate, having lost part of his foot. Nothing could be done to stop the incessant bleeding. He knew death was probable without medical attention. By supporting his weight on my skeletal frame, I managed to help. We jumped out of the blazing car. My clothes caught fire, so after safely clearing the flames, I rolled on the dusty ground to smother them. That first air raid ended, and I instructed my buddy to lie still until I returned. I made my way to the food storage car, helping myself to some bread, butter, and a little sugar. I then returned to my buddy's side; we ate all we could and I said to him, "If we are going to die, let it be with our bellies full." After that, once more supporting his weight on my own, we made our way to what were hopefully the advancing liberation armies. We saw some trees that looked like the entrance to a forest and proceeded. After making it about halfway, the RAF suddenly appeared out of nowhere and again started dropping bombs. We hit the ground with sudden instinct. A bomb exploded very near, projecting me at least twenty feet through the air. A dizzy spell reeled upon impact with the ground. I then felt something to the right of my head and turned to see directly before me a big piece of the bomb. An electrical sensation coursed my being. I shook my head in amazement by my luck in surviving such an ordeal once more.

I looked for my buddy and found him in a daze. We started for the forest again, and as soon as we reached the first trees, we took shelter. We planned to eat before anything else could happen. I had the bread wrapped around my waist and the butter and sugar in the bottom of my pants. I started to spread the butter on the bread to eat, despite the fear of the RAF dropping more bombs. Due to the proximity of the impacts, we were almost entirely covered with dirt. Our food was spoiled, but thankfully that was the last bombing.

We rested a while before starting for the presumed location of the British Army, but unfortunately ended up running into SS troops. They shuffled us back with the other surviving prisoners gathered from our convoy. The forest was our abode that night with SS troops encompassing us. My buddy and I escaped again but didn't get far before being recaptured. My buddy told me to try to escape by myself to increase probability of success, but I could not abandon him in his condition. "We will try again when it was darker," I assured him.

At about four o'clock in the morning, we attempted another escape, supposing success as we found deep in the forest an underground bunker for German civilians during British or American air raids. We meandered into the bunker, locked the door, and fell asleep from exhaustion until waking late the next day. We tarried in the shelter still in fear of recapture. We were awakened later that night by RAF bombs. They wanted to ensure nothing remained of the town, at least anything beneficial to the Nazis. After that raid ended, civilians searched for cover with nothing left but the shelter harboring us. Germans found us there and turned us over to the SS, and we again joined the others. Chance of escape was miniscule from that point in the absence of aid. Albeit, civilians by that time were afraid as well of SS troopers, who knew their war was lost.

In typical fashion, a formation was called the next morning to take a census of those still living amongst us. My buddy and I were the last in line as usual. We couldn't believe the final count: the remnant of 3,300 men and women amassed only a few days prior was 1,714.

Over the course of the bombing, the RAF killed countless scores of our own friends fighting for the same cause—people with an unlimited reserve of courage having made it thus far, annihilated at the hands of allies. I knew the death toll of thousands of innocent souls incurred by the RAF carrying out their mission would be suppressed.

That same morning, we began our march to Bergen-Belsen some thirty kilometers away. Bergen-Belsen was among the largest of Nazi concentration camps in Germany and certainly one of the most infamous. As tired as we were, the Nazis insisted we walk fast, but we just could not. Repeated beatings with sticks were pointless. We had to stop several times. Some of the SS were injured in the bombing and were also incapable of walking. One lost his eyesight. The putrefying sight of the blood-drenched soldier was sickening.

He begged for help to no avail. His commander would not help him; there were no doctors or medicine. While walking on the road, a group of French prisoners of war joined us. Occasionally, a French soldier encouraged us to keep the faith because liberation armies were advancing to eventually free us. We later encountered a number of other prisoners from Russia, Poland, and other countries. They said the same thing: "Hold on because the liberation army was coming."

We marched until dark then came to a forest and were finally permitted to lie down on the grass. The ground was damp from the previous rain, but wet or not was of little significance; sleep came instantly. We took to the road again at dawn with the camp not too far away. Finally after a little more struggle, we arrived at about noon that day. At first glance, the camp's appearance was inviting, previously serving as SS headquarters. We walked until told to stop in front of the crematorium, in front of which we stood for quite a while. Wild thoughts flooded our minds. We figured the SS would dispose of us since the Allies were so near, but some three hours later, we were somewhat at ease when the journey continued. We came to what was supposed to be our section of the camp. It was quite different from the previous section we had passed through. The ground was littered with bodies of unfortunate inmates. We stumbled with every step taken over a body. We continued walking about two or three kilometers and were halted by a guard. He informed us that if we had any intention of sleeping in the barracks we previously stopped in front of, we would first have to clean. Cleaning debris and dirt would have been a simple task—our clean up involved human debris. The barracks was literally piled to the ceiling with dead bodies. We removed the bodies through the doors and windows, dragging and dumping them into a huge pre-dug hole. The morbid task was finally completed by dark. Next, we had to fight among ourselves for a spot to lie down but relegated to be content with just enough room to sit. Sleep didn't come easily because some joker tried to steal my space. I was fortunate to have my buddy for assistance.

Five o'clock the next morning brought with it another task of cleaning more barracks in the surrounding area, but also ridding the area of body lice—they were colossal. This was a terrible task. Blood would backfire into our faces when one was underneath our nails.

The greatest portion of clean up in disposing corpses was impending. The SS ordered some men to dig a huge pit four kilometers from our barracks. We were forced to haul one body at a time and flop it into the pit. Despite the mere bones that were these corpses, none of us had the strength to carry out this task, so we soon stopped carrying the bodies. We searched for rope, cloth, or any other material serving the purpose of rope and tied it to the arms or legs of the bodies and dragged them to the pit. Two days elapsed and the task was by no means half complete. The restroom of the barracks was converted into a cemetery to accommodate the dead outnumbering the living. The bodies laid helter-skelter in the barracks, many adorning a sickly smile.

Water was sparse after the system was severed during the bombing, and eating was implausible. I was not feeling well and wanted to return to the barracks to lie down. It was then that I witnessed an episode that is assuredly unbefitting even for nightmares and will no doubt haunt me for the rest of my life. A fellow fell dead, and no sooner had he hit the ground when a number of guys from our group pounced on him, tearing him to pieces with bare hands and devouring him cannibalistically. Like vampires, others drank the very blood from his veins. I am ashamed to confess that I advanced to take part, but was knocked to the ground by someone fighting for the *food*.

I was in poor shape. I went to see my buddy back at the barracks; I was the only one whom he recognized. I could do nothing to help him, though. I simply reclined next to him as company. I was unable to get up the next morning, burning with fever, lice driving me crazy, and my buddy was comatose. I lost my mind that day, remiss of all sentience. This surely was to be the day of my passing, but something in me was stronger than iron.

Chapter 10

Liberty

On April 15, 1945, the momentous day of liberation by British forces, I passed out. My soul was ambivalent; all strength was depleted. I didn't recover consciousness until April 17. I first opened my eyes and saw the British and thought I was dreaming. I had begun to think the day would never come. I learned of President Roosevelt's passing from British discussion. He was instrumental to winning the war; we grieved the death of this respectable man.

My first day of freedom was not unlike the others—liberation was no guarantee that our lives would be preserved. The British were ill-equipped to help us right away. They inspected our barracks, looked around, and went away.

After fifteen days without food, our stomachs were bone dry. We were given meager rations of fat. Those of us who weren't dead or about to die were terribly sick. Late the next day, we were served canned food. I cannot explain exactly our reaction to the food in our hands. We were dismayed, as if having seen something for the very first time in our lives; I lost little time eating. I helped my buddy eat his and tried to offer some hope, reminiscing about the past.

The following day the British moved us to the next barracks, which housed some three-story bunk beds with a little better straw, but without blankets and still two men per bunk. Conditions were improved from before, but we did not call this freedom. I expected a doctor to come inspect us and try to save some lives. I hoped that at least he would look at those who needed medical attention the most like my buddy; I guess at that time the English didn't give a damn about us.

The fourth day after our liberation, my buddy died next to me during the night. I remember touching his cold body, holding him in my arms and crying my heart out; he had hoped for survival more than anything. His passing was unimaginable. He always looked forward to seeing his family again. He was not the only one: more than a hundred continued to die daily from dysentery and other illnesses.

The British took away my buddy and buried him just outside the barracks, then placed another fellow with me. This guy was from Belgium, but he didn't last too long, dying the following evening after a dysentery attack. The next day my new companion was an ex-captain with the French army. We had not received substantial care from the British thus far. A French chaplain came to see us once in a while and gave us some cigarettes and cookies.

One morning, I got up and tried to take a walk without clothing. The guy with whom I shared my bed loaned me some clothes to cover my nudity—clothes that he had obtained from someone else who had passed away. I went out and lay down in the sunlight. The feeling of relaxing without fear of beatings or torture was refreshing, to say the least. I went back to the barracks looking for the fellow who loaned me the clothes to return them, but he sat at the edge of the bed lifeless like the others—without warning. They took him away, and I crawled back into bed, awaiting my turn. Life was unchanging besides having food twice a day and as many cigarettes and cookies as we desired from the chaplain, but eating was unappetizing. Our desire was to return to our countries and homes, yet here we were still in the dirt. We had no idea when we would leave—maybe we'd leave in a few days or die like the others.

Two days later they gave me a new companion, but he died the same day, then one after another. In all, eight different guys died in my bunk next to me, and by some miracle I continued living. Remaining in my bunk was taxing—lice tirelessly nibbled my body. Even the white powder that was administered was of no use. I cracked the lice, counting each one until losing track after more than one hundred, so I quit. I remained in this condition until May 8.

That morning, a few ambulances stopped in front of our barracks. We mistakenly expected them for ourselves, but they were for any Russians lingering in our barracks. They told us our turn would be later. After three weeks of waiting every second of the day, however, we knew it not to be true. Each soul they took away in the ambulance was checked by a government representative of Russia. The guy sleeping in the bunk behind me said that he was going to try to get in the ambulance, rather than wait here to die. It wasn't too hard for him because he knew Polish. His family immigrated to Northern France when he was fairly young. His parents spoke Polish at home most of the time, so he knew the language pretty well, and since Polish and Russian are very similar, he didn't have a problem making himself understood.

Seeing him helped into the ambulance exhausted my patience; I tried the same. I saw a stretcher, crawled to it, and prostrated myself on it, passing myself off as a Russian; I figured this to be the best solution for survival. A Russian guy asked me some questions, but of course I could not understand him; the only words of Russian I learned in camp were the cuss words I would not use. I just moaned and rolled around on the stretcher like I was in too much pain to answer. Unable to extract answers, they assumed I was one of them and took me away in the ambulance to a destination unbeknownst to myself. I didn't mind. I knew it would be better than this barracks. We stopped about fifteen minutes later. They carried me into a building and laid me on a heated table, and then a German nurse—a prisoner of war—came over and bathed me. I gave her a rough time, telling her to shut her mouth as she spoke and ordering her to wash me over and over. The soapy water was glorious. I was so relieved to be free of lice.

Afterward, they placed me on another stretcher with clean white sheets, and then off I went to the hospital. They put me in a room with another young Russian man whom I could not understand. He didn't seem like a bad guy at all. Less than an hour later I received a glass of milk, bread, butter, and sugar. I ate this up in a matter of seconds and asked for more and received more. Then a doctor came in to completely examine me. He wrote a few notes down and asked me some questions. I weighed fifty pounds. I was just bones with skin covering my body—completely devoid of muscularity. The doctor was a German prisoner of war accompanied by a Russian officer. The doctor could not believe that I was still alive. He asked what region of Russia I was from. At that time I could converse somewhat fluently in German, so I told him I was French feigning Russian citizenry for admission to the hospital. At this stage their hands were tied, so I was allowed to stay.

I found a Frenchman in the hospital that same day. He told me to be leery of the doctor because he was a Nazi prisoner of war, and the British were merely using him until a doctor of their own arrived.

For a week we had enough to eat, but were without any quality medical attention. We were also restricted to the hospital grounds. I wanted to get out but lacked garments. Escaping to France on my own was senseless. I had to stay until they decided to send me back. We still were not free people. We didn't really have any more freedom than before, except we knew that we were no longer under the Nazi thumb. A few days later, unbeknownst to us, food rations diminished. It was shameful getting up at three in the morning like crooks—stalking garbage cans for food. Someone must have snitched because the next day the British forced us out of the room to search for the food hidden under our mattresses, but we didn't care, knowing the next night afforded the same opportunity. A few days later, which was the end of May—and a beautiful day—I was a few pounds heavier and decided to get out of bed and go outside for some fresh air. So with the help of two canes given by two British soldiers, I ventured out and basked in the sun.

As I sat under the sun near a window a few days later, I saw a French priest walk by. He was surprised to see me as I motioned to him. He approached, and I called the other Frenchman. The priest asked about what transpired; a radio broadcast in France had reported our survival, and I learned my brothers and sisters knew that I had survived. However, since several weeks elapsed without my return home, they had begun to doubt the report. They had hired a priest, who searched for me unsuccessfully, and assumed that I had died and was buried with the others. Of all of the close calls with death I had encountered over the past few years, this was my most promising day yet. The priest spoke with the British man in charge and returned to inform us that we would be leaving the hospital the next day in his custody. We did not sleep that night in anticipation of our return to civilization, where sneaking out in the middle of the night to eat from garbage cans was unnecessary.

We received some clothes late that next morning and were allowed to walk outside. At this point I was ten pounds heavier but still too weak to support myself. We didn't have to wait too long before the French priest came by in a car and took us to a building where all the French prisoners had been assembled for repatriation to France. We arrived a little late: a shipment had been sent back to France the night before, so we had to wait for the next. This was no hassle. The worst had ended.

However, eight days passed and life was not any easier. Stealing food was still necessary because the ration was inadequate for recovery. We snuck into a canteen for warm grub. Then the day we waited so long for finally arrived. It was like being born again—surviving the long-endured suffering, still whole; life completely changed. Past recurrent thoughts of death were replaced by assurance of being saved. In the late evening of May 30, word came that we were departing the next day for France. Understandably so, we did not sleep a wink again. We sang all night and I was already contemplating future endeavors. The morning dawned and about seven guys came in naming off twenty-four names, summoning us to be ready by nine o'clock. I was one of them and elated like never before. For the first time I can recall, I cried for joy.

I donated whatever I had to the guys staying behind. Then nine o'clock came, and we boarded a truck and departed. We drove through the city of Celle. Seeing Nazis standing in line at the grocery stores was pleasant to the sight. The tables had turned as they began tasting the bitterness we were fed. We stopped where the passengers boarded: a British installment with a landing strip. We lay down on the grass, watching the planes land, wondering which was ours. At about one o'clock, a C-46 landed in front of us. The pilot came over and said some had to wait. He had to go to Belgium first, so he took the women and the critical cases. I was not included since I was able to stand with crutches, hoisting my sixty-pound frame of bones. So, I went back to my spot and lay down on the grass, thinking about the luck I was having. Every time I was close to something there seemed to be something or someone interfering with it. A while later I took a walk with some guy to the British mess hall. The smell took us right to the cook, who was cutting some beef. I tried to get a piece, but our so-called liberators kicked us out. They treated us like criminals. Well, since it was not the first time, we were used to it.

By four o'clock the plane had not returned. They decided that we had to go back to camp, but no one would move. We insisted on staying a little longer, knowing that if we didn't leave that day, it would be some time before we would have another chance. At 4:30 they decided waiting any longer was worthless; we got back into the truck and were ready to leave just when we saw a plane that looked like the plane that had left earlier as small as a bird flying toward us. We leapt from the truck and ran for the landing strip, hoping it was for us. It was! The pilot rushed over and told us to start boarding. He did not have to tell us twice. We were all ready and the door closed, yet in my mind I would not believe until the plane left the ground. My skepticism was not unfounded. The pilot said maximum occupancy had been exceeded by four people, preventing takeoff. He said that he was authorized to take only twenty-four passengers, and with the two pilots, the radio men, and the women from the Red Cross, he had twenty-eight on board. They asked for four volunteers to go back to camp with the promise that they would be the first to go on the next trip. Naturally, we were all deaf to his plea and ignored him. One of the pilots opened the door and went out to talk to the truck driver. We knew he told him not to leave just yet because he would have to take four of us back to camp. I was scared to death because I was sitting close to the door. I was afraid that the pilot would pick the four men sitting closest to the door. The procedure differed, though. He took out the list with our names and said he would close his eyes and pick four names at random, and those would have to depart. There was nothing else for him to do. My heart pounded like hell until the four names were chosen. For once luck was with me, and I was spared. I felt sorry for those guys crying as they had to get off the plane.

Nevertheless, at about six o'clock the plane took off. While watching our plane leave the runway, I finally believed my dream had come true. The weather was spectacular, and the trip was pleasant. My face was glued to the window. I was also pleased to see that Germany had been thoroughly bombed. The women from the Red Cross gave us some food, but my mind was elsewhere.

Chapter 11

Home Again

A few minutes before nine o'clock in the evening on that fine, beautiful day, May 31, 1945, we landed at the Le Bourget airport just outside Paris. It was the first time in my life flying over Paris; it was mesmerizing. I didn't know whether to smile or cry. The door opened, and I was carried down from the plane. The French Army band lined up on either side of the door, and we were given a royal welcome back to France. The Red Cross took us to a reserved section of the airport. We were again served some food then put on a bus and taken to the heart of Paris, where a hotel had been prepared for our arrival.

Many people crowded the bus, asking for the whereabouts of their loved ones. We arrived at the hotel with some formalities to go through. A doctor completed a thorough examination, and we filled out paperwork and answered plenty of questions. Then we had our supper, the first real hot meal with all the trimmings. We were then escorted to a room with a really soft bed and clean white linens. Everything was wonderful like a dream coming true.

The next morning after breakfast we were each given a certain amount of money and some new clothes. We were free, free to do as we pleased without the scare of brutality. I had a hard time walking with my crutches, but they were necessary for support until I recovered. I didn't go back home, knowing nothing remained. The Germans had taken everything after my arrest. My father and mother were dead, and my remaining brothers and sisters were not in Paris.

I decided to visit friends—the parents of my friend Maurice who died in Auschwitz. They let me stay with them temporarily while I got back on my feet and began to reunite with family. I got in touch by phone with my brothers and sisters still in Meulan-Hardricourt, and a cousin came to visit me right away. I then stayed with his family for a couple of weeks until being sent away on convalescence for six months. I had gained too much weight too quickly after only two months, rising from 70 to 140 pounds. The doctor told me, "You blew up too much."

I took it easy the next few months, but instead of six months of convalescence, almost a year and a half passed before I was myself again.

Before Father was arrested, he had given some money to different individuals he deemed trustworthy for safekeeping and eventual disbursement to us children in the event of his arrest. I remember that he gave a 5,000 franc-note to a butcher with whom he conducted business. This man of exceptional honesty gave me the same bill he'd put away years prior, but every other person kept the money and avoided communication with me. They'd hoped none of us would return alive. I know for a fact that one individual in particular used several thousand francs to open a business, and I was powerless in recovering it. Father also hid money in other places, of which I was the only survivor privy to its whereabouts. He gave a butcher 5,000 francs, and had some hidden in our basement where coal was delivered for the stove that heated our home. The French government changed the currency in the middle of June 1945, but I was able to save a large sum of that money.

On June 4 or 5, four or five days after returning to Paris, I was finally reunited with my siblings, who were free in exile. Life hadn't been terribly pleasant for them in Hardricourt—as dull of a place as ever— with the family left in charge, who nearly enslaved them and squandered our money, presuming my parents would not be returning. I purposed to up my brothers and sisters as soon as possible and place them in an orphanage where they would be treated with decency and weekly visits would be possible. Seeing them again was the greatest moment of joy in my life.

Being one of the three survivors of the 1,500 sent to Auschwitz in our shipment, I considered myself one of the most fortunate people to ever live. However, I must admit that if the same situation recurred—if I were to be arrested, knowing what I know now—I would take my life immediately rather than go through that hell again. Many people were praising God for my freedom; I looked at them dumbfounded. While the majority of those praying to God for survival perished, I was determined by shear tenacity and will because they prayed to something that presumably did not exist.

Chapter 12

Recovery

Life was not exciting during my recovery, living in a very small village a few hundred miles from Paris in the south of France. Despite being two years out of the camps, all my strength was still depleted; I had none to perform any task. However, there was nothing to do. I was in a convalescent home near the Mediterranean Sea. French doctors believed strongly in the healing properties of coastal air.

I finally became independent and returned to Paris and filed a lawsuit to recover my father's business, which was sold to a Frenchman by the Germans. Fortunately, it didn't take long. I was awarded the business and a sum of money as punitive damages, which I never saw a penny of. Nearly twenty years old, I then went to court to be emancipated and sought the judge's approval without complication for guardianship of my brothers and sisters because the legal age was twenty-one. I took them from Hardricourt and placed them in a Jewish orphanage outside of Paris where they were treated humanely and received an education.

My brother Ben and I eventually reopened the shoe factory and the retail store, carrying a fair amount of fear of not knowing how long it would take to gain momentum. A friend of my father stopped by to see me; I was thrilled. We talked, and he promised to buy from my line, being a shoe sales representative, traveling often throughout northern France. I bought brand new equipment, hired several people, and commenced production immediately. The first months were relatively slow, but we suddenly received many orders, things were running smoothly, and life improved.

Ben, age seventeen, and I visited the children on weekends and brought their requests. Leaving was heart wrenching: Simon was fifteen, Joseph was thirteen, Renée was eleven, Thérèse was nine, and Jacques was seven. I didn't know what to do at that point. I knew that I couldn't run the business and care for them simultaneously. I wanted to make the best decision possible. Among the few papers and pictures that Ben saved was an old envelope dated early 1927. This letter was from an aunt of my mother, living in the United States. Here it was twenty years later. I wondered what the odds were that she was still alive and living in New York. I took a chance and decided to send her a letter. I explained what had happened to the family, and about a month later, to my surprise, I received a reply. I wrote to her in French, and she wrote in English. Translators were necessary on both ends. Her husband had passed away a couple of months prior to her receiving my letter, leaving her a dry-goods store. She was elderly; therefore, managing the store was burdensome. In her letter, she conveyed her sorrow over everything that we endured. My brother Ben and I started considering the benefits of immigrating to the United States to start new lives; surely it would be a better opportunity for the children to live in prosperity.

After much deliberation I wrote my great aunt back and related our desire to immigrate to America. I expressed that life for Ben and me was pleasant but not so for the rest of the children. We corresponded routinely, and she eventually decided to sponsor us, but agreed we would cover our own expenses. So I went to the U.S. embassy in Paris and received the necessary immigration paperwork. I sent all the papers to my great aunt's attorney to get the ball rolling. Meanwhile, I stared saving funds for our voyage. I was doing pretty well by now and did not encounter any problems. Before long, I was notified and permitted to make our reservations for the trip. I booked us on the Queen Mary for the spring of 1948. The passage had to be paid sixty days in advance. I didn't foresee any problems, especially the surprise awaiting us.

We went on with our lives, working and enjoying ourselves. I still had many nightmares and sleepless nights. Being free was sometimes surreal. Vengeful fantasies enveloped my mind of returning to Germany and machine gunning everyone in sight without regard for age or gender. I harbored hatred for the Germans. As far as I was concerned, they were all Nazis with pleas of ignorance merely enraging me further. I knew better. Violence against them was deterred by others' dependence on me.

Clockwise from the top: Bernard, Benjamin, Simon, Joseph, Renée, Thérèse. Middle: Jacques

Chapter 13

America

It was late 1947 when we received word that everything had been approved to leave France at our leisure. Ben and I decided to leave on March 10, 1948, allowing ourselves enough time to liquidate the business. We celebrated our last winter holidays and New Year in France with a bang. The time to pay for our passage on the Queen Mary came around; I went to the bank the evening before the sixty-day deadline and withdrew the necessary amount. The teller handed me 5,000-franc notes per my request, to avoid carrying a large bundle. We had finally accomplished our goal. We celebrated all night long, filled with gladness and joy, but the next morning brought the shock of our lives. God was surely against us again because the headline on the radio and newspaper said that anyone holding 5,000-franc notes was out of luck. That denomination of currency had been deemed worthless. I was in denial and took a taxi to the Cunard ship line and was the first one in line. I thought that perhaps the employees were not yet notified and would accept my money, but no chance. There were large posters everywhere exclaiming that the 5,000-franc note was unacceptable. I pleaded fruitlessly; canceling the reservation was not an option in my mind. Thankfully, they granted a thirty-day extension to pay the passage in full. I returned home and told my brother that we had to do something to raise the money in time.

The French government announced a few days later that exchanging two 5,000-franc bills for each member of the family was permissible. I salvaged 70,000 francs by exchanging fourteen notes. Then I used my head: I stood on the street and found a few vagrant drunks, took them to the bank, one at a time, and coaxed them into exchanging two bills each. I gave them a couple of bottles of wine as payment for their assistance. I remember recovering a little more than half the sum, but that was not enough. My father's friend (the one selling our shoes) agreed to loan me the balance. I promised to pay him back before leaving for the United States. I told him that my employees would be working a twenty-four hour shift and encouraged him to sell the shoes on the black market if necessary. I didn't care about legality; I was too close to realizing my dreams for my family. I then understood why Father never trusted French banks. I suspected that he had a Swiss bank account under a different name, but I was too young to be privileged to that information at the time. I also found someone to lease my business for a year with advanced payment. I figured to worry about the business later. I went ahead and paid for the voyage. Everything was going my way. I was able to repay everything borrowed and bought new clothes for us all.

March 10, 1948 finally arrived, and we departed from Paris. We took a train to Calais then a boat to England. We spent three days in London before boarding the Queen Mary in South Hampton. What a beautiful ship it was! It was like a city. Everything desirable was available. The five-day journey was not pleasant for some of my brothers and one sister, who were very seasick. They spent a lot of time in the cabin vomiting. I was not bothered; the time was pleasant. The extent of my difficulties entailed ordering food from our waiter. He was assigned to our table supposedly for his French fluency. Every time we asked him for something, he pulled out his little dictionary to translate. It was losing battle. We ate the best we could.

We're aboard the Queen Mary with our waiter en route to our new life in the United States. Left: Bernie, Jacques, Thérèse, Joseph. Right: Benjamin, Renée, Simon.

*A studio photo taken of my good side
at age 20 in France.*

We arrived in New York on March 18 to a most glorious site: the Statute of Liberty gifted by France, the city's skyscrapers, all of it was breathtaking. It was the beginning of a new life, new experiences, new language, not knowing what was facing us in this strange land, the hardship that we were to encounter, the disappointments. I guess we weren't prepared for it all. Maybe we were too young and expected more than what was to follow; we simply accepted our destiny to overcome whatever challenge confronted us. We exited the ship in the foreign and fast-paced city of New York. Our luggage was searched going through customs for whatever reason. I bought in France several bottles of Chanel No. 5 as gifts, for which I paid a hefty duty that offset the cheaper price. I thought someone would be waiting for us, but there was no one. We had to travel about 300 miles to Syracuse, New York. We were surprised to learn that New York is a state and somewhat large. When asking directions at the customs bureau, we were told to take a taxi to Union Station then a train to Syracuse. Two taxis were required to reach Union Station because the driver of one refused to transport the seven of us with our luggage. We waited for the train at Union Station and ate from a vending machine. The food was terrible, especially the white bread that stuck to the roof of my mouth. I was disappointed. We boarded the train for the six-hour trip to Syracuse.

We arrived at about 1:30 in the morning, hoping that my great aunt would meet us at the station, considering our oblivion to direction. We were actually met by her attorney and a couple of cousins of whom we knew nothing. I was able to converse a little in French with the attorney and spoke Yiddish with the cousins. My great aunt was unable to make the trip due to her age. It was cold and snowing upon our arrival to her house. We knocked on the door to receive her welcome. She opened the door and saw the seven of us. In shock, she refused to let us in. She thought I was the only one coming to work for her and take care of her business without compensation, thinking her good deed of me coming to America would be repaid with my enslavement. She apparently didn't realize the French are civilized and not greenhorns. The snow was unrelenting as her attorney begged to let us in for the night since it was late, adding that they would reconvene the next day to discuss the issue. Nothing could be said; she would not let us in. I didn't know how much of this I could take; my patience wore thin.

Finally after arguing back and forth, they came to a decision. The attorney said that he would take my two sisters home with him, the cousins would take two of my brothers, and the great aunt would let Ben, little Jacques, and me stay the night there.

This welcome was unreal. I told Ben that we should not unpack and just go back to France, but he insisted on waiting to see what would transpire. Jacques was afraid of the old lady. He held on to the loop of my trousers and followed my every step. We finally fell asleep for a few hours. In the morning, her attorney and the cousins were back trying to solve our problem because we had apparently become a problem. Things did not proceed favorably. The old lady didn't want any part of my brothers or sisters. She said she would keep me as the oldest, and I could work for room and board. I made up my mind that under no condition would I be her slave. It was decided that the attorney would keep my two sisters for a while and my cousins would take in my two brothers until a place was found for them. My little brother Jacques went to the cousin's daughter who had a boy about the same age, and Ben and I rented a one-room apartment in the city. I was enraged with the old lady and seriously entertained the idea of busting her head in, but Ben talked me down.

After that day we had practically no contact with her. Ben went to work at the cousin's brother's dry cleaning plant. The others started school; my future was undetermined. Finding decent work without knowing the language is easier said than done. I ended up washing cars for a while and went to the movies a lot to learn English. I attended evening classes for a while, but they were boring, so I quit.

Complications arose one right after another. The attorney's wife was diagnosed with breast cancer and required surgery, so he could not take care of his daughter, let alone my sisters. He asked the Rudolphs, a family with three children, to take care of my sisters until his wife recovered. They were a well-to-do family, the finest to be found anywhere. They were not only welcoming and hospitable to my sisters but to the rest of us as well. Shortly thereafter, the cousin's daughter also developed breast cancer and was hospitalized. Her husband labored, working and running to the hospital to see his wife. He hardly had any time to take care of his son and my brother Jacques. I sympathized for them both, having become close friends. Unfortunately, she passed away shortly thereafter at the age of thirty-four. When word got around, a family with a little boy asked to take Jacques, and my two other brothers went to a foster family. Ben and I, with the aid of others, did the best we could to support them.

Steady employment was scarce with my limited skill set in shoe manufacturing and knowledge of English. After talking with Ben, I was secure with the notion of the kids being in good hands and deciding on returning to France. But so many people whom I had met encouraged me, however, to not give up and allow enough time to adjust to my new life in the United States. So, at twenty-one years old I decided to join the United States Air Force to become more educated, learn the language faster, and obtain citizenship. I went to the recruiting office to pass the test that they were reluctant to offer me. One guy resented that fact that I was foreign, and a commotion ensued because I wanted to take the test, but another officer said that I had the right to take the test, leaving it up to me to pass or fail; I passed all parts with flying colors. The malevolence of the sergeant hindering me was obvious. I had a heavy accent; I'm sure he figured I didn't have enough language.

On September 17, 1948, I left Syracuse for basic training at Lackland Air Force Base in San Antonio, Texas. Basic training was no walk in the park. My life entailed rising up early in the morning, exercising, KP, and guard duty—a less than enjoyable experience. There was no reason to complain when comparing this dream to the nightmare that was life in the concentration camps. One morning, I didn't feel like going on a bivouac, so I snuck into the PX, and when my outfit left, I went back to my quarters to lie down. I was not the only one with the same idea. Of all the luck, a major and lieutenant came into the barracks for inspection. We jumped to attention as the major inquired of our estrangement from the others. He accepted no excuses and told the lieutenant to take our names for extra duties. He took all the names excluding mine. The major asked why he didn't take mine. He told the major that the day before I had gone on a hike and fell down and an ambulance brought me back to the base. I could not believe the lieutenant was covering for me because I didn't go on a hike the day prior, but I kept quiet. The major looked at my feet and said that I was unfit for the Air Force because I was 100 percent flat-footed. He told the lieutenant to place me on sick call for examination to determine if I should remain in the Air Force. I begged the lieutenant not to take me, but he said he had to file the report.

The doctor was congenial. He listened as I spoke about my desire to stay in the service to expedite my citizenship process and issued me a slip excusing me from all duties afterward. The first sergeant was waiting back at the barracks with threats for my misconduct, stating that I was in trouble. But before he could say anything else, I showed the paper issued by the doctor. He exclaimed that I had gotten away with murder.

I made many friends, some unable to comprehend my decision to join the Air Force after my experiences during the war. I maintained contact with my brothers and sisters by phone and mail. Everybody was doing fine. At the end of basic training, I was given a week's leave and had to report to Scott Air Force Base in Illinois after spending Christmas with my siblings. I stayed with Ben and saw the others every day.

The attorney's wife was not doing much better, so my sisters remained with the Rudolph family where they were accepted by the couple as their own, desiring to keep them as long as possible. The week vanished in no time, and I reported to my new base just before New Year's Day. Nothing much was happening because many of the airmen were on furlough. All I did during the holiday was pull some detail on guard duty and KP and clean the barracks. But I waited for the assignment I would never get—I wanted to go to language school to become an interpreter. I was instead assigned to the Headquarter Squadron and became a clerk. There wasn't too much to get excited over being in the Air Force at that time, it was simply routine.

About the middle of March 1949, I received a letter and documents. The family fostering my sisters and that of Jacques decided they wanted to adopt them; however, it was my decision to make as their legal guardian. I decided to discuss this over with the children for their reaction to determine if these arrangements were desirable. Even as young as they were, they understood the proceedings and wanted to be adopted. So I signed the papers and they became members of another family.

Of course, I never lost contact with them. Every time I went to Syracuse on leave, I would see my sisters and was treated like one of the family. It was different with my little brother Jacques. His new family asserted their adoptive authority, claiming that I should not have anything to do with him, but I resisted by all means. I was visiting him whether they liked it or not, but I was not able to see him as much as the others, a set of circumstances I'm sure my parents would have approved—we were acquiring a new language, the kids were adopted into good families. It just happened that Jacques's family considered him part of their family, not part of his old family. To say the least, it was hard giving them up for adoption, but I wanted to consider their opinions and sentiments, as well as conditions with those families.

I'm enjoying visiting my family while on leave in Syracuse, New York, September 1949.

Chapter 14

Family and Country

L ife persisted. I received several promotions and worked myself from clerk to chief clerk, the highest achievable military occupation specialty (MOS).

In May 1950, I met a girl, Charlotte, from St. Louis, Missouri, and was married six months later. I was supposed to be discharged from the Air Force on September 16, 1951; however, due to the Korean War, my enlistment was extended one year by order of President Harry S. Truman. I was released in August 1952, one month early because of accrued leave. I then decided to have the little amount of money that the French government had issued us for the death of my parents transferred to the United States, so

I went to the French Consul in Chicago for help. He handled my request, and about a month later, I received a reply stating that my request was denied because I was classified as a deserter of France and the money had been confiscated. When I inquired about this, I was told that I was being drafted into the French Army. I had never received any papers to that effect, and explained that I was issued papers precluding my military service for the time I spent in the concentration camps. Many years later, Jacques would go to Paris on vacation and enlist the help of a French attorney to resolve the matter. It took the French government thirty-five years to send me a letter of apology and inform me that the money had lost its identity.

In March of 1952, I applied for and received U.S. citizenship, becoming an American before the allotted time requirement. I changed my last name from Choroszez to Caron as a tribute to the man who lent to me the necessary funds to make our passage on the Queen Mary. He also worked diligently to sell the shoes I was manufacturing. Not to mention, no one in the Air Force could pronounce my name.

In October, 1952, my first daughter was born, Rhonda Lee Caron. Upon discharge from the Air Force, I decided to stay in St. Louis, where my wife's family lived. She had a brother, sister, aunt, and cousins. I went to work for her brother in his jewelry store. I worked roughly sixty-six hours per week: Monday, Thursday, Friday, and Saturday from 9:00am to 9:00pm; Tuesday and Wednesday from 9:00am to 6:00pm. I was off only on Sundays but sometimes worked on Sundays cleaning and trimming the windows. It was tough; I hated working for my hard-nosed boss. Every night I came home telling my wife that I wasn't going back the next day, but I had an obligation to maintain our expenses. My brother-in-law was probably the harshest boss I've ever worked for. He lacked all compassion. I guess he was greedy for gain at the time as his business lacked longevity and security.

Though I must admit that it was the best training I had ever received; I developed self-confidence those three years, learning also to never idolize money. Making enough to live a content life and to pay my bills was sufficient. I was not anxious to amass a fortune. I remembered what ambition did to my father and family. Obviously, I'm certain he would have made different choices if he could look into the future. Our personal and mutual sufferings resulted from misguided principles, possibly a similar outlook that may have drawn me back home during serious turmoil to be arrested and experience an incomprehensible brutality. The principles fundamental to our decisions seem to forge a path of particular possibilities—a roadmap of sorts that is quite accurate.

My family in Syracuse was doing well in the meantime. Ben had a lucrative position in a large department store then eventually became a VP for an insurance company where he worked for forty-two years. He recently passed away at the age of eighty. My two other brothers, Simon and Joseph, joined the Air Force after they finished high school. My sisters and little brother were excelling in school. They all attended college and were eventually productive members of society.

I worked in the jewelry store for about three years. I purchased my first house in 1954 in St. Louis County. My neighbors across from us became our best friends. Donald was a sales manager for a small insurance company. He told me about the job, piquing my interest. I saw greater potential than my gig at the jewelry store. The idea of working independently was definitely appealing. I quit my job, greatly upsetting my brother-in-law. He halted all communication with his sister and me for five months until realizing the opportunity to use me for part-time help over the winter holidays. Starting the new job was a challenging.

My second daughter, Debra Caron, was born May of 1955, and before long my income exceeded what I was making at the jewelry store. I stayed with the company only two years for ethical reasons. They were unreliable, constantly refusing to pay my client's claims. Despite my urgings, my clients were complacent in fighting for their rights. I eventually mustered up the nerve to quit and decided to go to work for the largest insurance company at the time. I took a sizable pay cut but figured to make it up shortly. My brothers and sisters were progressing back in Syracuse. Worrying about them was pointless; they were in good hands. I saw them every other year, and some visited me in St. Louis.

Everything was falling into place. My third daughter, Judy Michelle Caron, was born in May 1958. I was promoted to Insurance Consultant and continued success led to another promotion to sales manager a year later. I guess I was a workaholic, spending a lot of time away from home. I got along well with my immediate family but realized the lack of communication between us. I never attended the temple on Friday or Saturday, since I never wanted to talk about religion. My children didn't want to go to Sunday school, without my objection.

Personal entertainment consisted of attending professional football games; I only missed one in twenty-five years. We went out to dinner occasionally. My vacation time was mostly spent attending leadership conferences for the company, venturing off alone at times to play a little golf.

In 1966, I sold my house and bought a new four-bedroom in another county. Fixing up the basement and yard offered some activity during spare time. The kids were growing up fast. My eldest daughter graduated from high school and went on to junior college. She wed soon after. My second daughter graduated and then decided to become a chef. She enrolled in the Culinary Institute of America in Hyde Park, New York. After graduation, she attained a position at the Ritz-Carlton Hotel in Chicago. She eventually moved to southern California, and before long, she too was married. My last daughter, after high school graduation, attended the University of Missouri. While she was away, I guess I became kind of lonely and depressed. My work was about the only thing I cared for, and within time, that also got on my nerves, but I kept going for sanity's sake.

The years passed even quicker as I grew older, but bitterness and consternation over what happened during my youth lingered. I could not shake the scorn I harbored toward Germany. I would pack up my briefcase and walk out of a meeting anytime I came into contact with clients claiming German ancestry. I refused to do business with them. I also had explosive arguments at the office when I perceived anti-Semitism in other employees.

Something was missing from my life. The only person I could confide in was my friend Don. Unfortunately, he grew very ill and died soon after. I thought that I could confide in a supposed friend from the office, but as I met with him and his wife, they turned against me on Mother's Day of 1978, upset by my decision to separate from my wife. Charlotte and I typically got along; we just lacked common interests aside from raising our kids. We couldn't find anything to bond us together.

I met a young lady at work by the name of Julie. The first week she started working for us, we went out for lunch together with two other employees. I expected an amicable conversation. Instead, I was subjected to over one hour of banter about God and religion. I thought to myself, "This girl was let loose from the farm." I couldn't believe she could talk to me about God when I knew He did not exist. It was a boring lunch, and I was relieved to see it end. But somehow that young lady did appeal to me. There was something about her that captivated my thoughts. However, I kept my distance because I was still a married man.

Things started changing when we attended a three-week course on casualty insurance. We sat next to each other for lunch, and I was blindsided by love for this girl. It kept me up at night and on weekends as I thought about her constantly. I longed for Monday morning just to see her. We would see each other during the day purely platonically. We just talked and eventually grew fond of each other. She had been divorced for a couple of years and had two daughters, ages fourteen and thirteen. My life changed from that point. The void in my life was seemingly being filled. After I filed for divorce, Julie and I saw each other more often.

Chapter 15

Change

O ne Saturday morning just before Labor Day, I went to visit Julie. I arrived at her house as she and her daughters were leaving to go shopping for school clothes. They asked me to accompany them, but I declined and rested in their condo. I was alone that afternoon napping and had a clear vision of Messiah standing before me. I was in shock. I spoke to Him, verbalizing exactly how I felt about believing in God. I told him that I thought God let us down by allowing five members of my family to be exterminated by the Nazis. He subjected me to tortures, beatings, and starvation. He orphaned my brothers and sisters. Six million Jews perished in the war along with countless others. How could anyone believe there was a God? I kept telling Him off, declaring that I didn't want any part of Him, but He stood in front of me, listening to my anger. After I finished pouring my heart out, He looked at me with a love that enraptured my soul. It was incomprehensible.

He went on to explain the historical necessity of the Holocaust as the catalyst for the formation of modern-day Israel. This was astounding because I had no invested interest in Israeli affairs at the time. I arose to write some of what He spoke and returned to lie down. He continued talking, and I told him that I would think about our conversation but would not make any commitments. I was not about to be fooled after denying Him for more than thirty-five years.

He disappeared. I never forgot His face and appearance from that day. His hair was shoulder length and light brown with a small well-groomed beard. He had piercing blue eyes and wore a white robe. I saw Him coming toward me then from the chest up.

I fell asleep with a smile and feeling better than ever before. A few hours later when Julie and her two daughters came home, I told Julie what happened. She listened intently as I showed her the paper I wrote His words on. She was thrilled. She told me that YHVH loved me and wanted me "to be part of Him"—only the grace of God would bring peace to my being. However, I told her that I had not made up my mind and it would take more than that to alter my perspective. I guess what I was trying to say was that I was going to put Him to a test to verify authenticity. He came to me several times after that first encounter. We talked a lot, and I tested Him. What I asked of Him eventually came true. Prayers were answered: I didn't know if it was coincidental, but it did happen. I needed to know more about Him, so I started reading the Bible little by little. I also started attending church services on Sunday mornings. The pastor spoke of the Jewish heritage that all Gentile-believers partake in, which was very much appealing. However, I was still very disturbed, because as a Jew, I was not supposed to accept Messiah as God. I always preached to my brothers and sisters that the Gentiles were responsible for the murder of our family in the Holocaust. I battled to reconcile conflicting thoughts storming my mind for many restless nights. I needed so much more time to determine whether this was real or just a dream. Yahushua offered his companionship practically every night. We talked about so many different things for several months.

I was so troubled by what was happening that I neglected my work; I had a lot of problems to cope with. My divorce was in process, and my kids couldn't understand what was happening to my mind. Many people told me I was losing my sanity. My ex-brother-in-law suggested that I see a shrink because he thought I was going insane. I took his advice and told him to pick the psychiatrist. I wanted my brother-in-law to choose to increase the likelihood of his belief in the results of the analysis. He told me he would pay for the visit since it was his request, except I told him to forget it because I did not want to accept any charity.

He made an appointment for me, and one week later I went. I spent an hour with the psychiatrist; we talked, and he asked me a lot of questions, which I answered honestly. At the end of the session he asked me point blank, "Why did you come to see me?"

I told him, "My family thinks I'm crazy for what I am doing and they recommended you to me."

"Go tell your family that there is nothing wrong with you," he answered.

That same evening, I stopped by to see my ex-brother-in-law. He was glad to see me because he thought the doctor confirmed my insanity. I was happy to inform him of the doctor's assessment. He became sarcastic and did not believe me. I told him to call the doctor and find out for himself.

I know now that I needed that appointment. My mind and soul were relieved of much tension. One night, shortly thereafter, something happened inside my body. I had burning sensations in my chest and face. Yahushua appeared again, and I accepted him as the Messiah. I was born again. A huge weight had been lifted from my chest, and I experienced profound joy.

In March 1979, Julie and I were married. I moved into the condo with Julie and my two stepdaughters, Shelly and Kelly. Since Julie and I worked, we only took that weekend off to get away, figuring to honeymoon later on.

We went to Wilderness Lodge, located on the Black River in southern Missouri. The word wilderness was not an exaggeration. The lodge was located on thousands of acres with a few cabins without a telephone, television, or radio. I was ready to go back home, but Julie was persuasive. The next morning we found out that we were the only two on the premises until that evening. The next morning, while eating breakfast, the entertainment director asked about our prospective itinerary and suggested several things; we picked canoeing.

I had never been in a canoe on the Black River, so I didn't know what to expect. I was dressed in slacks, dress shirt, leather loafer shoes, and a long leather coat in 20-degree weather—not exactly appropriate for canoeing.

Another couple also decided to canoe. Their decision proved to be miraculous. We were led upriver about five miles from camp. The driver put the canoe in the water and gave us life jackets as required by state law. Since it was so cold, we used the life jackets as cushions. The other couple took off first.

As our canoe circled in stagnation, Julie yelled, "Bernie, use your paddle like a rudder." I didn't reply, so she yelled again. I then asked her, "What's a rudder?" She knew then that we were in trouble. We eventually made forward progress but headed directly for a tree that had fallen into the river. Julie used her paddle to push us away, but we capsized. My feet could not touch the bottom and my leather coat was pulling me down. I came up for the second time and could yell for help in a panic. The other couple's attention was caught, and they came to our rescue. They both jumped in the water, the man pulling me safely to a nearby sandbar while his girlfriend pulled

Julie out. Bob rushed us to remove our clothes. Julie was startled and answered back, "I beg your pardon!"

"Take off your clothes before you go into shock," Bob clarified.

The four of us undressed and we walked in a circle to keep warm. We then introduced ourselves in the buff. Bob said to me, "I see that you are Jewish, so am I!" Julie asked me how Bob knew I was Jewish; I told her it was because I was wearing a mezuzah around my neck. After an hour, we wrung out our clothes and got dressed. Julie was given long underwear by Lois. Bob asked if we knew how to canoe the Black River. We replied with a negative. He took the lead; I would canoe with him, and Julie would ride with Lois.

Our belongings were stored at the front of the canoe to dry and we departed. There was no trouble for about two or three miles, then we reached an area where two fallen trees formed an arch over the water with just enough space for our canoes to pass under. Bob and I went first with ease, but the current knocked Julie and Lois against the stumps, incapacitating the canoe. Bob suggested going back and helping. As we approached, the current drove us into their canoe, turning both canoes over. I surfaced and swam safely to a nearby shore. I watched Bob, the canoe, and our belongings float downriver. Bob reached a shallow area and stopped. In the meantime, Julie was holding onto a branch and would not let go. Lois yelled for her to let go or else freeze to death. Julie still would not release. Lois kicked her, forcing her into the water, and both were at the current's mercy. Bob was in the middle of the stream and able to grab them, and pull them to safety.

We were forced to remove our clothing again, and we started walking in a field of dried corn stalks, which caused cuts and bleeding. The woman of a couple that had been fishing saw the overturned canoe along with our belongings floating down the river, she jumped into their old car and drove up the dirt road, knowing somebody had to be in trouble. Thankfully she found us wondering around, naked and dazed. Coincidentally she had just done her laundry, so she had a basket of clothing in her back seat. We covered up with sheets and other garments. She took us back to the lodge, and I reported the incident to the owner. He sent one of his drivers to recover our belongings, if possible. Julie and I got to our cabin, took a hot bath, packed our car, stopped by to express our thanks to Lois and Bob, and checked out from the lodge. The owner told us that the driver was able to recover the two canoes, but the rest was lost. I had to pay him for the life jackets, a small price to pay in contrast to still having life. Our shoes, my leather coat, and the other things were gone, but who cared about it. This was a test that YHVH passed. Maybe this had to happen so that I would know if I could depend on Him without losing faith as I did before.

Summer approached quickly, and we had to make arrangements for Shelly to go to summer camp in Burlington, Vermont, as was customary for several years. Shelly was excited to go, eager to see her friends and compete in activities with the other campers. She was exceptional in horse competitions, having already won about two dozen ribbons. We let her go despite limited funding. She left late July for about a month. We received letters from her and called her. She was happy there.

In August we attended my nephew Steven's bar mitzvah in Schenectady, New York, and decided to extend the trip a few extra days to visit Shelly afterward. We first stopped overnight at Julie's parent's home in Dayton, Ohio, and then went on to Schenectady. Kelly was with us.

The bar mitzvah was fantastic. I only wished that my sister Renée could have seen her boy that day. She died in 1975 at the young age of thirty-nine from breast cancer. We left the next morning for Burlington and arrived late in the afternoon.

Shelly was waiting for us after informing her that we would be arriving soon and was thrilled to reunite. We went out for dinner and she spent the night with us in the hotel. We took her shopping the next day and then took her back to camp. Only a few days remained until camp ended; we asked her to come back with us, but she insisted on staying to finish riding in the horse competitions. So we left and stopped in Dayton again for a couple of days on our way home.

The next day, Julie's mother, Julie, Kelly, and I saw a movie at a shopping mall and heard a page over the intercom but disregarded its relevance to us as we headed out. Julie stayed with Kelly to do some shopping for school. I took her mother back home because she wanted to do some cooking. As soon as we pulled into the driveway, my father-in-law came out running and crying. I was baffled as to what was going on. He regained composure and informed us that the camp called with notification that Shelly was in an accident. She was hospitalized in Burlington, Vermont, but the hospital would not release any information over the phone.

I drove right back to the mall to find Julie and Kelly. By that time they had heard their name called over the intercom, and a police officer had told them to get back home quickly. I ran into the mall and saw them running toward me. Julie thought something had happened to her mother. I told her on the way home that Shelly was in an auto accident and that we did not know the extent of her injuries. Julie almost fainted. She thought something terrible might happen if Shelly stayed. Immediately after arriving home, we called the hospital, but they still would not divulge any information.

I called several airlines to see if we could get a flight out, but no luck. We were willing to drive to Chicago, Cleveland, or Cincinnati just to get there the quickest way possible. None of the connections could have gotten us there until the next afternoon. We decided to get in the car and drive straight through.

Julie, Kelly, and I left immediately. We stopped several times on the way to call the hospital to hear there was no change. After an exhausting night we arrived at the hospital around noon. We saw the surgeon in charge immediately. He told us in plain language that the prognosis did not look good. Shelly was in a coma having sustained severe brain damage. They operated on her skull to release the pressure. We waited as she was supported by a respirator. We could only pray and wait.

The next day we went to the police department to find out more about the accident. We were told that a young counselor from the camp borrowed a Jeep and asked several girls to go play miniature golf. There were six girls; Shelly was among them. On the way to the course, he took a winding road, and according to witnesses, he was driving too fast. We don't know if he was trying to show off or what was on his mind, but he lost control and veered off the road. He tried to recover, but swerved across the highway, bounced off a tree, and rolled several times. The driver and five girls were thrown, but Shelly was pinned under the Jeep. An off-duty paramedic coming from the opposite direction saw the accident and tried his best to help Shelly, but she was unconscious. She was transported to the hospital in Burlington and admitted to intensive care with around-the-clock care. She was hooked up to several machines. It was heartbreaking to see her that way. All we could do was pray and ask our friends and family to do the same. For eight days we paced the hospital floors. It was so nerve-wracking that I started smoking again after having quit for fifteen years. I had put my trust in YHVH and hoped that He would pull her through, but eight days later, on August 24, 1979, the doctor told us she was brain dead. He advised having the respirator disconnected, but before they did, they wanted our permission to remove her kidneys to save the life of someone else. We did a lot of thinking and praying as to determine the right decision. At four o'clock that day, we gave them the okay to remove them. We asked them to call us at my sister's house in Syracuse to update us on the functionality of the kidneys. The doctor promised he would.

We left Burlington for Syracuse. We arrived at about midnight and soon after received the call from the hospital that everything went fine and that the kidneys were in good condition. Two lives were saved with them.

We spent the night at my sister's and left for Dayton early the next morning to make the funeral arrangements. She was buried next to her grandfather, who also died in a tragic accident just about the time Shelly was born. We left Dayton the next morning for St. Louis to resume life, which was not pleasant for several months. Julie was in a very depressed state. I was concerned that she may have a nervous breakdown. It is hard to explain what we were going through; we kept praying and asking YHVH, "why, why, why?"

It seemed so tragic because Shelly was such a delightful person. She was so kind and helpful to everyone she came into contact with. She was a pleasure to be with, and to this day, we cannot forget the tragedy that struck. It changed our lives tremendously. Julie blames herself for having the respirator disconnected. She cannot accept the fact that Shelly died and no one could have done anything about her condition. Her memory will always be with us.

Julie had to change her profession. She left the insurance industry because she could no longer face families and talk about their product—compensation for the loss of a loved one; death became all too real to her. She went to work for a major freightliner. The long hours were quite demanding but worthwhile in retrospect because she needed to stay busy.

I helped her with the evening entertainment she was obligated to. It was fun eating out—at first—several nights a week in the finest restaurants. We attended baseball, football, hockey, and soccer games, plus movies and theater, but like anything else, the lifestyle became mundane, especially when having to entertain folks who were not pleasant to be around. We also had golf outings, Western parties; Christmas was a big event.

I learned in May of 1983 during our trip to Paris that my mother's cousin Sarah had promised my mother that she would look after her children if anything befell her. I was unaware of this promise and did not keep in touch with anyone in Paris. I had a new life in the United States and just wanted to put the war and everything about France behind me. Unbeknownst to me, Sarah had been trying to locate my brothers, sisters, and me for more than thirty years. She was happy to see me and was also mad at me for not keeping in touch. She expressed her grief to me for being unable to keep her promise to my mother; I was sorry in return, but there was nothing that could be done to remedy that situation. I did try to make amends by staying in touch with her and her children for the rest of her life.

Sarah died at the age of ninety-nine. She cooked meals for the elderly and sick until she was ninety-four years old. All of Sarah's children were successful in life and married with children. Sarah was embittered by the holocaust. She forbade her children to marry a Christian; although one of her sons did so. Consequently, she neither saw nor spoke to him for forty years. Sarah liked my wife but was ignorant of Julie's Christian faith. Sarah could see how fond Julie was of the entire family and reciprocated. Sarah's daughter Lisette implored her to see her disowned son, but she refused, declaring that she would never have a Christian in her home as long as she lived!

Lisette then told her that Julie was a Christian. This must have softened her heart against her son because she agreed to invite him to her house to meet his wife and their son. All of the years could never be recovered, but my cousins rejoiced in the embrace of their brother as family.

I became ill over time with angina, completely oblivious to the diagnosis until finally visiting the doctor on December 9, 1983, who recommended that I see a cardiologist. I had a client that was a cardiologist, whom I had known about twenty years, so I had no problem scheduling an appointment. I took a stress test and tallying test. As soon as the doctor saw the results, he called me at my office and told me to get to the hospital within an hour. I told him that I could not leave my unfinished obligations to clients. He insisted on dropping whatever I was doing and rush to the hospital. He told me he would be waiting for me there. I could not get in touch with my wife, so a co-worker drove me on a Tuesday afternoon before Christmas.

I remember being admitted on Tuesday and waking Sunday morning. My wife was at my bedside as I writhed in excruciating pain. She let me know that I underwent a quintuple bypass open-heart surgery. They say I would not have survived the passing of Christmas; they could not delay the surgery. All the medication did not mitigate the pain. I would have chosen death had I been offered.

Life's complexion takes on a particular shade after experiencing uncommon extremes. The significance and meaning of each untimely experience are unique. I find little to no association between my time in the camps and later infirmity. Some may speculate that the body must have developed fortitude to withstand such conditions. I'm not sure about that, but I do know that I was bound by Germans for entirely different reasons than being bound by a failing heart.

I was hospitalized until New Year's Day, 1984. I was incapacitated by the frigid weather. I was to take short walks but couldn't go outside. The cold knocked me off my feet; I could only walk around inside our basement. My chest hurt intensely, preventing sleep and also suppressing my appetite. I lost twenty pounds and struggled day after day with pain. The bones in my chest wouldn't heal. After several follow-up visits to the hospital, the original surgeon said that I had to be readmitted to the hospital so they could rewire the bones.

My chest was reopened and rewired in April. I have never been the same. I was in constant pain and had no quality of life.

Julie and I contemplated for a long time and thought my life was now limited and uncertain. The doctor's prognosis was 18 to 24 months to live. In July 1984, we sold our house and decided to do some traveling. We bought a fully equipped recreational vehicle and decided to travel all over the United States. We sold our house and one of our cars and left St. Louis for Dayton, Ohio, to spend two or three weeks with Julie's father. It was my first time driving such a large vehicle. I was not at ease thinking about the inherent difficulties traveling across the United States would bring, so we decided to sell it.

We stayed in Dayton until late November and decided to move to California where I would enjoy kinder weather. I arrived in California on December 2, 1984, and Julie joined me for Christmas. She went back after New Year's 1985 to aid her niece who was sick in Columbus, Ohio. She returned to be with me and start an entirely new life in late January. We purchased a new home in Laguna Niguel.

Chapter 16

Desired Relations

We looked for fellowship in our area and found a church that we liked. Connecting with civilized individuals was simply our natural inclination. The Sunday morning after a damaging and fatal earthquake hit Mexico, we assumed our minister would take up a collection to facilitate immediate help. Instead his sermon that day was a bit egocentric. He passed out paper and pencils and asked us to write down what we would like to acquire within a year, such as a car, a boat, a new home, etc. He said "we have not because we ask not." The look on the faces of several parishioners conveyed bewilderment; we realized that we were in the wrong place and never returned.

We then found a nice, quaint church in Dana Point with a minister who was approachable. It seemed a coincidence, but two ladies who happened to be Jewish and were married to Christian men who attended the previous congregation had also ended up at the same church. They were also dismayed by the affairs at the previous church, and had departed that church the same time that we left. We got to know these ladies over the course of several weeks and became friends. As Passover approached, one of the ladies organized a successful Passover Seder in the church with the minister's permission. It was something that the people were interested in knowing more about, and more than 250 people attended!

We were blessed there until the following year's Passover; we planned another Seder and collected money for the meal. The results were terrific, even more people wanted to attend the Passover Seder. However, the minister changed his mind and refused to permit use of the building. He had received complaints from other parishioners objecting to the

Seder, claiming it was too Jewish and unnecessary to observe annually. The minister refused to refund the money that had been collected for the Seder meal and deposited it into the general fund. We presented him Scripture commanding the observance of Passover for all generations. He just brushed us off and dismissed us by saying "that there was a golf outing planned for that weekend." We left without returning. The anti-Semitism was chronic.

The lady organizing the Seder was determined to bring the message of the Gospel to Jewish people as well as Christians who were unaware of the significance of keeping Passover. She formed a fellowship called the Olive Tree Connection; we met once a month in her home. There were between forty to fifty people, Jews and Gentiles mixed. It was the best thing that could happen. This lasted for about three years. A Messianic-Jewish congregation grew from this group of believers. Many of the initial people in this group moved away from Orange County, but we remain good friends to this day.

Our group of friends went to Jerusalem for the Feast of Tabernacles in the fall of 1987. It was a ten-day excursion—the first three spent touring Israel, visiting many ancient sites referenced in the Tanakh. We also visited the Sea of Galilee and the site where the Beatitudes were preached, and then finally ventured to Jerusalem for the Feast of Tabernacles. The tour leader explained that we needed "dressy clothes" for the event, as it was being held at the Binyanai haHuma in Jerusalem, and Prime Minister Yitzak Shamir was going to address the group of people, about 5,000 Christians from around the world. Of course we had left our "dressy clothes" in Tel Aviv the first night of our trip! We frantically called the hotel, hoping they could ship our clothes to Jerusalem, but they claimed they did not have our clothes. Julie said to me, "Let's pray about it, after all we are in Jerusalem; we should have a direct line to the Almighty from here!" We prayed. It was time to go to the event—no clothes.

After the opening night's activities, we found our way to our bus among fifty other buses resembling ours. We were sitting on the bus waiting for everyone in our group to arrive, when I looked to the front of the bus and saw a man holding up a clothing bag, shouting "Bernard Caron." Miraculously, our clothes wound up on the bus with a man who spoke no English; we never found out how our clothes found us.

The three-day celebration of the Feast of Tabernacles, sponsored by the International Christian Embassy, proved to be a spiritual turning point in our lives. Old Testament scriptures came alive for us; we began to understand the Hebrew roots of the faith and saw the clear connection between YHVH's feast days and our Jewish Messiah. Julie especially marveled. The beauty of our faith was unfolding before our very eyes!

Julie wanted to stay in Israel; she felt at home. So we decided to return the following year for the Feast of Tabernacles to tour Israel on our own. We rented a car and drove to the farthest northern point of the tiny nation, a town bordering Syria called Metula. We met and were invited to lunch by a Christian family dedicated to prayer, who had been living there for several years. Times were peaceful when we visited Israel's border with Lebanon; the Lebanese were led by a Christian government for many years, but conditions were changing. People everywhere were friendly; many invited us into their homes to dine with them. We were at home.

Getting lost in Beersheba and the scorching heat thwarted our plans to visit Eilat. We turned north to Shefahim and stayed a few nights on a kibbutz right on the beach—not exactly the Ritz-Carlton, but they served three meals a day and had a swimming pool with perhaps 100 feral cats, which are everywhere in Israel—no need to worry about mice or rats.

I am normally on guard and vigilant but actually laid back while in Israel. We relaxed, enjoyed ourselves, and swam in the Mediterranean Sea. Julie noticed that I was in my element, not worried about anything or anyone. This further convinced her that we should make Israel our home.

We celebrated the Feast of Tabernacles in Jerusalem with about 5,000 Christians from more than

70 different countries; the celebration was organized by the International Christian Embassy in Jerusalem. We also participated in a parade through the streets of Jerusalem with more than 25,000 people, most of whom were Israeli. People from all the different nations were asked to dress in costumes native to their country. Since we lived near Disneyland, we decided to dress like Mickey and Minnie Mouse! We marched through the streets of Jerusalem, throwing candy to the Israeli children who were screaming "Mickey, Mickey!" with delight. They ran after us, clamoring for our mouse ears after the parade. Little did we know that Disney is quite popular in Israel, especially Mickey Mouse. It's an experience that will be treasured for the rest of our lives. The Israeli's were joyful to see so many people from other countries carrying banners in support of their beloved land. It was difficult leaving again.

Our lives were gradually changing. We began observing the seventh day Sabbath and enrolled in a Hebrew class at the local college. We eventually moved to Riverside County and started attending a Messianic-Jewish congregation in town. We were learning so much about the faith and looked forward to Shabbat every week.

We continued with this congregation for several years, but a huge division manifested and things fell apart. The congregation split, and we were heartbroken. Individuals with a Protestant background formed a separate congregation, and those of Jewish heritage maintained the original congregation. We found ourselves again out of fellowship, neither inclined to continue with the Christians nor with the Jews, despondent with the unreconciled conflict between our brothers and sisters. We remain cordial with all of them, but we were not compelled to continue with either group.

We searched for fellowship, attending several congregations, but nothing lasted long. Most congregations we attended had problems with weak leadership and disorder. The Messianic movement is such a diverse group of people emerging from a plethora of faiths, seeking the truth of the faith of the Messiah. Tremendous infighting resulted from divergent perspectives blended with an unwillingness to take more time for consideration and mutual understanding. This movement attracts people hungry for more truth of their Messiah, but it seemed everyone had their own idea of how services should be conducted. Jews tended to want more "Yiddishkite," and Christians wanted services to be just like church services except held on the seventh day instead of Sunday.

The shame I witnessed in the camps again cannot be compared to such inhumanity. I'm referring more to the shortsightedness of individuals claiming to care for one another. Despite being distant from prisoners in the camps because of a fear to lose companionship, there was still a common bond uniting us—hope for liberation. Followers of the Messiah would claim to possess a common hope for a peaceful future as well, although oftentimes, peaceful temporal conditions leave room for ourselves.

We planned a vacation to Hong Kong and China in early 1991. Before we left, a friend gave us the name of someone to contact in Hong Kong. A few days after arriving in Hong Kong, we got in touch with the individual. He was a minister and requested that we take some Bibles to Chenzen. We agreed, fully aware that importing Bibles was strictly prohibited by the Chinese government.

We met two fellows the following morning, one from Australia, and the other from Oklahoma. They gave us two large suitcases for delivery to a hotel in Chenzen. We followed their instructions, no questions asked. We crossed the border into Chenzen without a problem, delivered the suitcases, and returned to Hong Kong.

A message waited on our phone the next morning, requesting delivery of two suitcases to Canton. We picked the suitcases up the next day. This was not as easy as the first trip. We had to cross the British border as well as the Chinese border. We stood in line for hours waiting to cross the British border, only to find out that we needed a visa to cross the Chinese border. We had to stand in line to get a visa, and then stand in line again to cross into China. Julie had no problem crossing the border and waited for me on the other side. A Chinese guard told me to place my suitcase on a conveyer belt to be x-rayed. I set my overnight bag on the conveyer belt, left the suitcase on the trolley and tried to wheel it to the other side to wait for my overnight bag. The guard stopped me and said "put bag on belt." I said it was too heavy to lift, so the guard picked it up and put it on the conveyer belt. Halfway thru the x-ray machine the belt stopped; the guard examining the suitcase opened a dividing curtain and asked me in broken English, "What you have in suitcase?"

I replied, "Stuff."

"What kind of stuff?"

Again I said, "Stuff." (I wasn't about to tell him "Bibles.")

He said to me, "You have books."

I sarcastically retorted, "So what?"

He came around from the other side—with the help of another guard—picked up the suitcase, and emptied it onto a table. I was amazed to see the amount of Bibles unloaded. I also had a waist pack that he made me take off. He looked inside and found a beautiful leather-bound Bible and threw it in the trash. I reacted, "Hey, that's my personal Bible!" So he retrieved it, opened it, looked inside, and asked, "You read Chinese?" I denied that, explaining that I collected Bibles from every country I visited.

The conversation wasn't going well. Both guards carried me by my arms into a room where another Chinese guard waited. As they yelled at me in Chinese, I shouted back, "Yell at me all you want, I don't understand Chinese." I exuded courage while my stomach harbored fear. I was not afraid until one of them yelled "passport," which I had to give up. For nearly two hours I sat in discontent; they were yelling, and my thoughts cycled: "What is going to happen?" They eventually returned my passport and released me. Julie was waiting for me in the shadows with the two guys, who gave us two more suitcases before we boarded the train for Canton.

The train was crowded that Chinese New Year. Canton was a madhouse when we arrived—wall to wall with people. Everyone was pushing; drunks were strewn in the gutters in rivers of urine. The Chinese were about our size: focusing on the tall Australian was our task. Without knowledge of our destination, separating from him would present a precarious matter.

I was separated from Julie and could not find her, so the Australian and I went to the hotel where we would spend the night. He left the suitcases with me and went to look for Julie and the other guy, finding them after several hours of searching. Needless to say, I was worried. We had not told anyone what we were doing; no one in the world knew of our whereabouts. I tried not thinking about what might happen if we were arrested and held without the ability to contact anyone. No one would even know where to look for us.

They returned, and we spent the night in the hotel with only minor issues. The food they served in the restaurant was unappetizing. I wouldn't eat it and bought some candy to fill myself until we returned to Hong Kong. With quite a bit of difficulty we were able to get return tickets on the train to beautiful Hong Kong, where we enjoyed the rest of our vacation.

Chapter 17

Back to Israel

After returning home, we decided to host a group of friends observing the Sabbath. The times entailed reading Scripture and conversing about various matters, but we missed corporate worship and fellowship. Convenient timing brought word about a group of Christians going to Israel to volunteer in the Israeli Defense Forces. There were about thirty-five people from different Protestant denominations in the group and only three Jewish people in total, all of which were believers in the Messiah.

We spent three weeks in April of 1995, exactly fifty years after our liberation a week and a half following Passover, working on all sorts of projects on a medical base outside Tel Aviv and to celebrate Passover. We lived with the soldiers, wore the same uniforms, and ate the same food at the mess hall on base; food that was very different from what I was used to in the States. Tomatoes, hard-boiled eggs, and cucumbers were a typical breakfast; cucumbers, tomatoes, and lettuce for lunch; cucumbers, tomatoes, eggplant, and chicken for supper! It was pleasant if cucumbers, tomatoes, and eggplant were your taste. The Israeli soldiers were amazed by our work ethic and wondered what prompted us to leave the comforts of the United States to work the harsh conditions of an Israeli Army base. It was an edifying experience. Everyone got along; we all had the same objective, and we put our denominational differences aside, working as one. We wanted to help the Israeli people and wanted to show them the love of Messiah.

Living conditions were especially difficult for the women. All sixteen of them were together in a rather large and open room with bunk beds and no dividers for privacy. With so many people coming and going at different times of the day, it was difficult to keep the door closed to keep insects out, and the mosquitoes were fierce at night! So Julie tried to motivate the women to remember to close the door when they left. She told them a story from our first few months of marriage.

Since we both worked outside of the office in sales, we could sometimes get away in the early afternoon and go back to the condo for a little "afternoon delight." As we enjoyed each other I said, "Je t'adore, je t'adore."

Julie replied, "The girls are in school."

I thought it a strange reply, and again whispered playfully, "Je t'adore ma cherie." Julie abruptly got up, and I asked, "Where are you going?"

She replied, "I'm going to shut the door!"

I was baffled: "Why? The girls are in school."

"You told me three times to 'shut the door ma Cherie.'"

I then realized she didn't understand French, and I explained that "Je t'adore" means "I adore you." We had a good laugh.

Julie told the women in her barracks the story, provoking laughter and fixing the problem of keeping the door closed in a peaceful way. From then on everyone imitated my suave sophistication with "Je t'adore ma cherie." It made the rather grim accommodations much more cheerful.

General Davidi invited me to speak to the camp about my experiences in the camps during the Holocaust. It seemed more than coincidental that this was the fiftieth anniversary of our liberation from Bergen-Belsen. The world had a conscience. We were able to return to our homeland, and here I was, sharing my testimony with my kinsmen, who were without conscious memory of not having a homeland. One soldier asked me, "Why didn't the IDF do something?" No sooner after he had asked the question, he realized the IDF had not existed. The land being restored to Israel is redemption for those who lost their lives and definitely a miraculous gift granted by our Father in Heaven. No other nation that I know of has been exiled for 2,000 years from their home to be later restored and established.

*Julie and me sitting to her left in the front
row while volunteering with the IDF.*

We returned home; Julie was displeased about
leaving Israel, but I wanted to travel to different countries and was motivated to return to Paris where I still
had several cousins who survived the holocaust. They
were never taken to concentration camps during the
war, but their father was taken to Auschwitz where
he died.

We flew back to Paris in 1994 to visit family for
a few days and then rented a car in Paris and headed
to Switzerland to stay for a week. We drove through
southern France and stopped to visit with Lisette

and her husband, Henri, who retired to Cannes. We stayed in a cousin's beautiful villa for a few days and indulged in a few memorable meals on the Riviera.

It is amazing in Paris and on the Riviera; people bring their dogs with them even to the finest restaurants. After finishing a wonderful meal in a very nice restaurant on the Riviera, we were leaving, and a dog peaked out from under the tablecloth. We were shocked to see a dog in a restaurant. Dogs and cigarettes, a common site in a French restaurant!

After leaving the Riviera, we stayed in Bordeaux a few nights and toured several of the region's famous wineries. We went to Biarritz—close to the Spanish border—and did some sightseeing.

Meanwhile, Julie just couldn't get Israel out of her mind, wanting to go back, so we decided to return for the fall feasts. We planned to stay for three months to check things out and make a decision about moving to Israel and becoming Israeli citizens.

In September 1996, we rented an apartment in the German colony in Jerusalem. For a long time I harbored resentment toward Germans, though our landlady became our dear friend almost immediately. She made a cake for us every Shabbat, and we gave her flowers. The time was endearing with a closeness of family and a mutual love for the land. Shabbat was like nothing we ever experienced. By 3:00pm on Friday, everything was closed—no cars or buses on the road, the entire city was at rest. We were invited to friends' homes every Shabbat, then at sundown the following evening—like a cork coming out of a champagne bottle—the entire city buzzed with activity. Cafes and restaurants opened, and by 8:00pm, people were drinking coffee, having a nice dinner, or visiting family. It was fascinating to watch Israelis stay up past 1:00am then rise up prepared for work the next day. They are truly an amazing people, friendly and full of life. It was not unusual for our neighbors to knock on our apartment door at 10:00pm, asking for our company at a café for coffee and conversation. They would wake up at 6:00am, go to work all day, come home and fix supper, and then were ready to go out to relax with friends and repeat the whole process the next day.

We lived in Israel for three months without a rental car; the bus was our primary mode of transportation—which turned out actually to be a blessing. We grew intimate with Jerusalem. It was not unusual to walk down Ben Yahudah Street with passing cars honking and occupants waiving, calling us by name—a rare phenomenon in the States.

Going to the shook to shop for food was unforgettable. The shook was an open-air market with everything fresh—from the bread to the chicken. Shopping on Friday was customarily crowded with folks awaiting the bus, especially around 2:00pm since the last bus to run until sundown Saturday night was scheduled for 3:00pm. One particular Friday, we were pushed aside several times when the bus came. Others mobbed the bus, and we were left standing there while another crowd of people gathered to wait for the next bus. Julie told me "we're getting on the next bus." Evidently Julie doesn't know the Israeli formula for pushing people aside. After pushing our way onto the bus, a lady yelled at Julie, "What's the matter with you, don't you have any manners!" Julie apologized, and we had a good laugh at home.

We took the bus to the Dead Sea but got off at the wrong stop. We didn't know that this wasn't exactly where we wanted to be, so we caught the next bus and went a few more stops. We got off at the sight of some nice hotels and decided to have lunch right when Julie realized that she left her purse on the bus. She was afraid I would be mad, but unable to resolve anything, we simply enjoyed lunch together. We happened to catch the bus back to Jerusalem and asked the driver if anyone had turned in a purse. He became animated: "So you're the one who left the purse on my bus!" He directed us to get off at the next stop and wait for the next driver whom he would have deliver the purse to us. So we got off and the next driver brought the purse with nothing missing. We decided to stay at the Dead Sea for a few more hours and catch the last bus back to Jerusalem. Unbeknownst to us the fall schedule had started that day, and the last bus to Jerusalem was the bus that delivered Julie's purse! We waited at the bus stop in the middle of nowhere; the presumed scheduled time came and went, but no bus. It was getting late but not dark because a glorious full moon was out over the Dead Sea. A lady paused when she saw us at the bus stop and told us that there were no buses to Jerusalem until the next day. She offered to take us to En Gedi to try to make it before the last bus left for Jerusalem. We made it just in time! This was commonplace during our time in Israel. We lived spontaneously and were always protected. Julie loved being there and felt at home, but I longed for the comforts of the United States.

We took another trip by bus to Eilat, stayed for a couple of days and crossed over into Egypt to visit some sites during our stay. We don't know whether it was because we crossed the border in Eliat, but the environment was less than inviting. We also went to Petra, Jordan, to see the amazing city built in the side of a mountain; the narrow path into the city is only accessible by walking or by donkey, designed as a haven from outsiders. The traveling was gratifying, but Julie was glad to get back to Jerusalem.

We were invited by friends in Jerusalem to an orthodox Jewish wedding—an unusual experience for us. The bride and groom took their vows under the chuppah and consummated their marriage immediately after the wedding in a small cottage, while the guests waited in the reception hall. The men were on one side of the hall with the women on the opposite side of a curtain partitioning the groups. The festivities commenced upon the arrival of the bride and groom, the men and women remaining separate.

The passing of Chanukah marked the time for our departure. Friends threw us a going-away party. A genuine shared love made our departure back to the United States particularly difficult. They did not want us to leave, and Julie definitely wanted to stay. As much as we hated the thought of leaving, the timing was not right to make Israel our permanent home. Our Israeli friends will not be forgotten. Julie keeps in touch with them to this day.

A consistent highlight of our trips to Israel is Yad Vashem; every time is surreal and so impressive, memories forever etched in my mind. I can never help but to weep upon entry of the memorial to the children with names and ages posted. My throat clenches at the sight; I cry.

It is always pleasing to visit this plaque at Yad Vashem memorializing my family members that were killed during the Holocaust. This tribute in some manner conveys sentiments exceeding my ability to utter.

Chapter 18

Division

U pon returning to the States, we decided to attend a local Conservative Synagogue. We were warmly welcomed by everyone and began to attend regularly. My wife was very active in Hadassah, even becoming president of the local chapter. We didn't try to hide our faith in Messiah; I was hoping to introduce my brethren to the love Messiah showed me, attempting to dispel misconceptions they may have learned about the Jesus Christ they had become acquainted with across generations of prejudice and persecution inflicted by the Church. My relationship with Messiah proved to me that he was mischaracterized by people taking God's name in vain through foolish act. The Messiah of the Scriptures won me over with an unconscionable, unsurpassed love that I know is extended to others.

A troublemaker told the rabbi that we were *Jews for Jesus* trying to convert people in his congregation to Christianity. This was a blatant lie; we had no association with *Jews for Jesus*. The rabbi instructed his congregation to shun us. This was heartbreaking and surprising; I had never seen Jews behave in such a manner. It's our custom to welcome the stranger. I was hurt for Julie because I knew how much she loved these people. The vitriol directed toward her was unnecessary. She loved all the women in her Hadassah group. She was simply thrilled with the opportunity to be among them and extend the love of Messiah.

What is the world coming to? I had been hated by so-called Christians because I was a Jew, and now I was hated by Jews because I had accepted my Jewish Messiah. My world was turned upside down! I then began to understand what Messiah meant when he said "the foxes have holes, and birds of the heaven *have* nests, but the Son of Man has nowhere he may lay *His* head."[4] We had been thrown out of the synagogue and cut off from our longstanding relationships. It was as if we no longer existed to the people that we considered friends. We were disenfranchised once again.

Julie began to look for a place to fellowship with like-minded believers, but I insisted on not getting involved with another congregation. I was happy just keeping Shabbat with my wife and minding our own business. Julie kept up with Scripture and Hebrew study but became glum without fellowship with other believers; I conceded, and we began worshipping with another local Messianic congregation. Everything was going smoothly, and we became close to these brothers and sisters in Messiah.

This lasted for several years, but of course, division sprung up again within this congregation. The heartache is difficult to imagine without experiencing an ugly schism, especially in such an intimate setting, a setting designed for camaraderie. Countless scenarios account for such conflict, but these usually deduce to pride. We sometimes forget that something may be wrong with us at any given moment—perspective, beliefs, judgments, character; apply the same situation to those you're dealing with, and you have a recipe for disaster, either side potentially exalted beyond reasonable measure. It is important to be certain of and rely on sound principles, discriminating between good and evil; however, knowing versus understanding and implementing are entirely separate matters.

We now fellowship with only a few people in our home. It is distressing to find so much of men's dogmatism within both church and synagogue. Such traditions teach many things foreign and contrary to the Scripture, dividing people. To top things off, either side accuses the other of the same offense! I find it ironic to have been walked the course of life God has paved, to end up observing such calamity within the community of believers in YHVH. Yahushua of Nazareth warned us about the traditions of man and was persecuted by religious authorities because of obstinance toward their foreign teachings. He was a revolutionary, who offered himself as ransom so we may be redeemed from our transgressions against the Creator and defilement of the creation, preserving us from Heaven's wrath to know the joy of dwelling with our Father in His glorious eternal kingdom.

Chapter 19

Parting Thoughts

S ix million Jews died in the holocaust, and the world was temporarily shamed by the blatant anti-Semitism that had been waged against us across the centuries, and then Israel became a state in a day. After 2,000 years Jews at last had a place to call home. It seems the pieces are falling into place for the Day of YHVH. Before this happens, persecution will abound against those whose only crime is worshipping the God of Abraham, the God of Isaac, and the God of Jacob, having accepted the offering made on the tree by Yahushua haMashiach and turned from worshipping themselves and other idols, calling upon the name of YHVH, believing in Yahushua as master and savior. It is time to put our pride and arrogance aside, repent and turn our hearts toward God, serving one another, preparing for the return of the Messiah.

Many people wonder how a Jew who suffered at the hands of so-called Christians could accept a gentile messiah. The Messiah as portrayed by many has taken on such a complexion, but the Messiah of the Scriptures, the One that I know, is of the tribe of Judah, the Son of David. He is neither a Catholic, nor a Christian nor does He practice Judaism. The Word delivered His law to Moses, and then observed and taught it infallibly. He is one with our Father in Heaven—the only hope for mankind.

I am now eighty-four years old and not in good health. My days are uncertain, so I have to answer a final question: over the years I have been asked what I would like to be remembered for. I don't have to think about it, but if I answer, there is not one, but two things. First, I survived the camps only by the grace of the Almighty. Second, finding my four brothers and two sisters in the same village where they had been hiding during the war was worth more than words can describe. The opportunity to make decisions for the betterment of my family after the war and in the United States was a privilege and honor.

End Notes

Forward

[1] Dwight D. Eisenhower Memorial Commission, Washington, DC, 2004 "Ike and the Death Camps," [http://www.eisenhowermemorial.org/stories/death-camps.htm], June 2011.

[2] Ibid

[3] Ibid

Chapter 18

[1] Matthew 8:20

CPSIA information can be obtained at www.ICGtesting.com
Printed in the USA
LVOW07s0402061115

461280LV00027B/158/P